Photographing Airplanes

Photographing Airplanes

The Art of Aviation Photography

Steve Mansfield

HOWELL PRESS

For Jill.
For patience, indulgence and inspiration.

Published in North America by Howell Press, Inc.,
700 Harris Street, Suite B, Charlottesville, VA 22901.
Telephone (804) 977-4006.

Library of Congress Catalog Card Number 91-70476

ISBN 0-943231-43-4

Printed and bound in Singapore by Kyodo Printing Company (S'pore) Pte Ltd

First Printing

HOWELL PRESS

CONTENTS

ACKNOWLEDGEMENTS

The biggest thanks must go to my wife Jill, for her excellent contribution of ideas, advice and photographs, and for her patience and indulgence during the hours of being deafened by aeroplanes and the days of being alone as I hid in the office, sweating over a hot word processor.

I must also extend my warm thanks to George Hall for his advice and help, his hospitality, and his unselfish willingness to divulge the secrets of his trade. More power to your Nikons, George.

Likewise, my gratitude goes out to Norman Pealing for his time and enthusiasm, and for showing me what can be done with a Hasselblad and a strong faith in your seat belt!

Most of the material for the profile of Charles E. Brown comes from the two-volume collection of his work, *Camera Above the Clouds*, compiled and edited by Anthony Harold (published by Airlife, 1983 and 1985). Anthony Harold is a curator at the Royal Air Force Museum, Hendon, which houses the Charles Brown collection, and was extremely helpful in supplying prints for this book. The two Brown books, lavishly illustrated with examples of his work, are a fitting tribute to the phenomenal talent of the photographer, and are highly recommended to newcomers and experienced photographers alike.

My good friend Doug Selway undertook the unenviable task of reading the original manuscript. His invaluable suggestions concerning structure and content contributed a great deal to the final product and I can't thank him enough. And the same goes for the timely contributions of Henry Pack. Naturally, any mistakes which remain are entirely my own.

Many people gave me hints and tips which I'd overlooked or which confirmed things I wasn't sure about. These kind folks include BIXen rsimonsen, dhudes, benvensite, and bozlee, and CIXen bhewart.

Finally, I would like to thank Alastair Simpson for giving me the chance to do it.

Picture Credits

All photographs are by the author, except:

Jill Phillips:	Pages 21, 35 (left), 67, 69 (left), 76, 77 (top and bottom), 83, 90, 94, 97, 99, 118, 136, 137, 139 (right)
George Hall:	Pages 59, 61, 63, 64, 65
Tony Holmes:	Page 109 (right)
Norman Pealing:	Pages 128, 129, 130, 131, 133
Charles Brown:	Pages 147, 148, 149, 150, 151, 152 (Courtesy of RAF Museum Hendon)

FOREWORD

People have been taking pictures of aeroplanes ever since the first machines lumbered into the sky. Even on that chilly, blustery day in December 1903, when the Wright Flyer clawed its way into the air in the world's first controlled powered flight, John Daniels was there to trip the shutter of Orville Wright's camera.

There are many reasons for photographing aircraft, from recording auspicious moments to creating mementoes of a pleasant day at an air show. The machines themselves almost beg to be photographed, resplendent in arrogant colour schemes, soaring through dramatic skies.

Well, it's not always like that. If it were, the aviation photographer's job would be a lot easier. Aircraft can be surprisingly difficult to photograph. Shapes which look stunning and graceful in the air take on awkward and ungainly proportions when you try to arrange them in a frame. A gorgeous, cloudless sky becomes a minefield of exposure problems. An aircraft on the ground is invariably set against an ugly background of lamp-posts, power lines and factory chimneys, or is hiding behind barriers, surrounded by people; yet when it takes to the air it is far away and moving fast.

These are generalizations, of course, and life isn't always that bad. But even when it is, there are techniques you can use to eliminate, or at least alleviate, the problems.

There are many reasons why you may be reading this book. You may be an aviation enthusiast wanting to use photography as a way of recording what you see, to get more out of your hobby. You might be a photographer looking for new and more exciting subject matter, but unsure how to tackle it. You might run an air taxi firm and want to take pictures for promotional use. Or you might be the owner of a warbird, looking to get some pictures of your pride and joy. Whatever your reason for being here, I hope you get something out of this book.

Of course, that diversity of readership does have its problems. A keen photographer, for example, will already have a reasonable camera outfit, and will know the basic techniques. However, even the general sections of the book have been written with one subject in mind — aircraft. And that subject can provide an unexpected twist, often changing, or even reversing, normal photographic practices.

So in these pages I hope photographers will learn how to modify their techniques and adopt new ones, and discover what extra non-photographic skills are needed, and what equipment to use. And for the photographic novice, whose interest is simply in photographing aeroplanes, I hope this book will provide enough information and inspiration to get you started — if your interest in photography grows there are plenty of books available to teach you the more arcane intricacies of the medium.

This book is not intended to be a dry and highly technical manual. I hope you will read it cover to cover, learning along the way. There may be things you will already know, depending on your level of experience, but you may also get a few surprises.

There is a belief among many people that 'equipment maketh the photographer' — which, roughly translated, means that to get the best shots you need the best equipment. On the whole this is a cop-out: you can get good pictures with any camera. However, it has to be said that with tricky subjects like aeroplanes, a well-stocked kitbag is going to be something of an advantage. Consequently, I have devoted the first main section to a discussion of the best types of camera, lens and so on.

One thing which is certainly true is that we can all learn from the professionals. For that reason I have included interviews with two of today's top aviation photographers — George Hall and Norman Pealing — and a profile of one of the pioneers, Charles E. Brown.

I have assumed a familiarization with the more basic photographic terms and concepts. The important ones are covered in a glossary, but if you've never picked up a camera before, it may be wise to invest in a simple primer book first.

The biggest compliment you could pay this book is to put it down, as I hope your imagination and enthusiasm will be stimulated enough for you to want to stop reading and start taking photographs. Enjoy!

Steve Mansfield
London, 1991

INTRODUCTION

FIRST CATCH YOUR AIRCRAFT

The most difficult thing about photographing aeroplanes is finding them in the first place. Then you have to get near enough to photograph them. The ease with which you can solve these problems depends on the country you are in and the depth of your pocket — after all, if you can't get close enough to someone else's aeroplane, you could always buy your own. Failing that rather radical solution, what are your options?

AIR SHOWS

Air shows are useful in that they get you close to aircraft you would otherwise stand little chance of seeing, particularly warbirds and military types. And the crews are there to show off their aeroplanes, which is good news for anyone trying to get interesting shots.

The catch is that you often can't get quite close enough. Static aircraft are usually roped off, and during flying displays you are kept back behind a barrier — to keep you safe and the organizer's insurance premiums down. Flying aircraft are kept a certain distance from the crowd line as part of the safety regulations imposed by either the military authorities or the local aviation regulatory office, such as the Civil Aviation Authority or the Federal Aviation Administration.

Fly-ins and meets tend to be more informal, and you stand a better chance of getting close to the machines. If you have a silver tongue (and perhaps a bottomless bank account) you might even get a ride. You are unlikely to come across the more exotic or macho machines, but that might suit you.

The obvious place to find aeroplanes is at an airport, which occasionally has viewing areas

There is one less obvious benefit from air shows. People with families or partners whose interest in aircraft is — to say the least — marginal, can use the excuse of a good day out, keeping the less enthralled members of the party happy with the sideshows and general festivities while indulging in their favourite pastime.

AIRPORTS

Most large airports have observation areas where you can watch aircraft taxi, take off and land. And with a suitably long lens, there are rich pickings for the aviation photographer.

Alas, the situation is not as simple as it used to be. Concern over terrorism has led to many such areas being closed down. Photography inside terminal buildings is usually banned, and it is frequently forbidden to take pictures anywhere in the vicinity of the airport.

In spite of the general suspicion of photography by airport staff, it is sometimes possible to obtain permission to take pictures. Contact the information desk or public liaison officer to find out how to do this. It is a good idea to telephone before you go, even a couple of days beforehand, in case there is some red tape to go through. Offer to show examples of your work as proof that you are a genuine photographer.

Even if you can't get on to an airfield, getting close might be enough. Watching a few take-offs and landing approaches will tell you which is the active runway, and it's quite likely that there will be a road or public area along or beside the flightpath from which you can get excellent shots. Once again, be careful about doing this in sensitive areas or around military bases.

The main problem with airports is that your view may be restricted and the aircraft some distance away. This Douglas C-133 Cargomaster was shot at Anchorage during a refuelling stop

Incidentally, if the take-off or approach is being flown specially for you, arrange a height with the pilot at which he or she should pass your position or, better still, an easily recognisable landmark such as the perimeter fence. This could save you from a nasty shock, as the speed with which aircraft gain height is widely variable, and you might find yourself looking at the wrong piece of sky.

The more city-bound photographer needn't despair. Although major airports are usually out on the perimeter of cities, heliports can often be found right in the middle. You might even be able to get on to an adjoining building for a more interesting angle.

Light planes at flying clubs and
FBOs can make interesting subjects
if you're prepared to work at it

Below: Museums can be a good source of subjects, often rare machines you won't find anywhere else, although being stuck inside with distracting backgrounds can be a problem.
Right: Some museums have exhibits outside where background interference can be minimised

AIR BASES

Not surprisingly, staff at military installations are even less fond of having photographers wandering about. Yet people still try it, partly because it is often so easy to walk on to the less secure military bases that it doesn't feel as if you are doing anything wrong. But you are.

The armed guards are there for a purpose, part of which is to introduce you to the delights of having cold steel pressed up against your ear while you lie spreadeagled on the ground — should you venture too far with your camera. That, of course, is if you are lucky.

Even if you are on an airbase for a legitimate purpose, such as visiting an air show or museum, it is unwise to wander off and explore the rest of the installation. Stick to the areas deignated for the public.

The laws vary from country to country, but the general rule is that unauthorized photography is banned, and not just on the base. In the UK, for example, taking pictures of the outside of a military

Below (left): As well as getting you close to aircraft you wouldn't otherwise see, displays also often provide an excellent variety of types.
(Right): Air shows are possibly the best source of interesting and vintage aircraft, especially warbirds

installation can put you in breach of the Official Secrets Act, in all its controversial glory. This, in turn, can leave you languishing for quite some time in one of the country's many penal institutions. Elsewhere, whole regions may be closed to photographers, especially in the vicinity of NATO or Soviet air bases.

The pictures you see in magazines of military aircraft and bases — aside from those taken at air shows — are usually shot either by military personnel or by professional photographers who have worked hard to make sure they have the proper authorization. This can take a lot of time and red tape to obtain, and is unlikely to be granted unless you are taking pictures for a purpose — a specific book or magazine article — and have letters of accreditation from the appropriate editor to prove it.

The other side of the coin is that if you do get permission, it is usually the key to the red carpet treatment by the crews and operations people, who love to show off, and an unparalleled opportunity for picture-taking. It's just that it's tough to get that far.

LOCAL FLYING CLUBS

Clubs can be extremely good value. If you are lucky, your local club may have the odd interesting aircraft lying around. But even if you're stuck with a collection of dull spam cans — the usual motley array of Cessnas and Pipers — at the very least you'll get plenty of practice. It's quite possible to hire an aircraft or two, with pilots (flying with your knees while taking photographs is generally frowned upon by the authorities, although it is done). This can work out to be rather expensive, however.

Your best bet is to cultivate a few tame pilots who might be willing to take you along when they are going up anyway. It is, of course, strictly against the rules for pilots without commercial licences to accept any kind of reward for their flying. On the other hand, if you really want to buy some fuel to put in the aircraft, there's probably little they can do to stop you. And you'd be surprised what some people will do in exchange for some nice, glossy 10 x 8-inch prints commemorating the event.

At the very least, local airfields tend to be less suspicious of photographers than their large, international cousins. It is still not advisable to go wandering around by yourself, for your own benefit if no one else's. Pilots coming in to land tend to be somewhat rattled when they find a photographer strolling along the runway. And you could wind up with an awful headache if you get in the way of the prop.

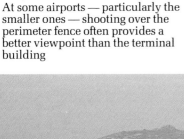

At some airports — particularly the smaller ones — shooting over the perimeter fence often provides a better viewpoint than the terminal building

MUSEUMS

It might seem like cheating to shoot aircraft in a museum — like fishing in an aquarium — but aviation collections do provide a valuable source of rare types. They are especially good for close-up work — details of engines, markings and so on. If you are lucky, you will find the aircraft parked out in the daylight where they are easy to shoot. If they are stuck indoors there can be a few technical problems, lack of light and colour casts from the artificial lighting

Below: Military air bases provide opportunities for great shots but getting permission is difficult

Left: If you are allowed on to a military airfield, you'll probably be escorted everywhere, to make sure you don't see anything you shouldn't and don't get in the way of operations

being the main ones, but nothing you can't overcome with a little care.

The only real drawback is that you are rarely alone. The most beautifully composed shot in the world is easily ruined by having some gawking tourist walking into the background. Later on we will discuss how to deal with crowds, but the best approach is to avoid them altogether: try to get into the museum when it is normally closed.

Many museums, or parts of them, close down during the winter months. This can be a good time to visit, if you can arrange the necessary permission beforehand. Often you will find the exhibits, particularly the flyable ones, being worked on, and this can provide excellent opportunities for close-ups, and shots of engines and parts not normally on view. You can also get pictures of people working on the aircraft — sometimes they can be as interesting as the aeroplanes themselves. If you are allowed in, and this applies to private owners who have allowed you into their hangars, too, consider it a favour, and one you might like to repay with copies of the pictures.

Local airfields and flying clubs may not have the most exciting aircraft, but they are accessible

GLIDERS AND BEYOND

If you are not obsessed with fast jets and other types of heavy metal, you might like to think about gliders as a subject. Somehow, the pure bliss of sailing the thermals translates well into photography. These (generally) elegant machines demand the same techniques as powered aircraft — and so are useful for developing your technique — but are easier to handle because of their slow speeds. It is much less hazardous strapping cameras to the outside of gliders than it is with high-performance jets. They are also much more accessible. Gliders tend to be based at small air strips, away from the busy and security-conscious main airports. And they are flown by people who are in it purely for pleasure, and may be better disposed to help you. As they are cheaper to run than powered aircraft, you are more likely to be able to catch a ride. And if you do have to pay for flying hours, it is less likely to break the bank. The same also applies to microlights.

Below: Museums have good collections of interesting and rare aircraft, although the environment is not always ideal. Lighting can be especially tricky with colour shots

Left: Museums are also notorious for cluttered backgrounds, and you may have to be prepared to wait for crowds to clear

There are gliding and microlight clubs which are often part of normal flying clubs, and they should be your first step. As with an ordinary club, contact the group and let it be known what you want to do.

Although your main interest is probably in getting pictures of the better-known types of aircraft, don't rule out less conventional modes of flying. Hang gliders, balloons and even kites can provide a useful training ground for techniques — particularly remote control photography. And once you've mastered the techniques, they can provide a means for getting thrilling and unusual pictures.

Whenever you photograph, watch out for small details. The shot is likely to look better (and possibly sell better) if the aircraft has been tidied up — 'remove before flight' tags taken off, ground equipment cleared away, tie-down ropes and sun shields removed, canopy closed, and that kind of thing. Naturally, you will need the owner's permission to do this, but it's worth seeking out. And think about the environment in which you're photographing the aircraft. If you must have something in the background, it's better that it is a hangar than a housing estate, and sea planes always look more natural in the water than racked up on the shore.

When there's nothing much happening in the air, and you've done about as much as you can with static aircraft, think about turning your lens on to other subjects on the ground: crews, support equipment, fire trucks and so on. If you want to sell your pictures, additional details such as these which flesh out the story will make your work more attractive to potential clients.

Finally, make friends! Frequenting a particular airfield, offering to help with odd jobs and chores such as pumping fuel and cleaning aircraft, could win you photo opportunities not normally available. Many pilots are happy to exchange a little air time in return for your labours. And even if you don't want to go that far, knowing people on first name terms always helps.

Above (top): Other forms of flying can provide opportunities for great shots. Gliders present most of the same challenges as powered aircraft, but are often more accessible

(Bottom): Getting a ride on a hot air balloon might be easier than in expensive power aircraft. And special events, like the Great Reno Balloon Race shown here, are just begging to be photographed

(Opposite): Even shot from the ground, balloons are invariably photogenic.

EQUIPMENT

The hardcore photo enthusiast is not hard to spot in a crowd. Just look for the person resembling some weird kind of technological Christmas tree, festooned with more bits of modern hardware than the average airliner flight deck. You may also notice that this person spends more time fiddling with the camera controls and gadgets than actually taking pictures.

It is all too easy for photographers to get hung up on equipment, at the expense of their pictures. Yet in aviation photography, the kind of equipment you use has a direct impact on the pictures you get. That's not to say that you have to spend a fortune on kit — although it helps — but you should choose your gear with care. We'll start by looking at the basis of any outfit — the camera itself.

THE CAMERA

Below (right): Compact cameras are very portable and highly automated, although they can be restricting. Some now feature short range zoom lenses, but you can't change lenses and exposure control is limited. (Left): Top line professional SLRs have all the necessary features, are robust and have the best system backup.

You can photograph aeroplanes with any camera, with varying degrees of success and ease. Owners of simple pocket or compact cameras may sometimes look with envy at the professional's abundant kitbag. But try lugging that bag around an airfield on a hot day and you will understand why the professional sometimes looks with envy at the simple cameras of snapshooters.

That said, it is true that the more sophisticated the equipment you have, the greater the variety of shots you can attempt. Without question, the best all-round camera type for this kind of work is the 35 mm single lens reflex (SLR). It's portable, takes a wide range of lenses, has a large accessory system, uses high quality film and is fairly inexpensive — at least, it can be. Indeed, an SLR is almost essential if you want to get at all serious about taking pictures of aeroplanes, and much of this book assumes that you are using this type of camera.

However, before we get too carried away with the virtues of the SLR, let's take a look at some of the other types of camera you can use, and their relative merits. We'll start with the simplest.

POCKET CAMERAS

Pocket cameras take 110 cartridge or disc film. They are small and light, which means you don't mind carrying one all the time — you need never be without a camera. And they are cheap. If you want to experiment with strapping cameras on to aeroplanes, it's not a bad idea to start with an Instamatic — that way you won't be too heartbroken when it falls off at 1,000 feet.

Of course, the real reason these cameras sell is that they are easy to use. The only work you have to do is press the button, and maybe decide whether the weather is sunny or cloudy. Yet that simplicity is the major downfall of the type for aviation work. The camera has a fixed wide-angle lens; if the aeroplane is to be anything like a decent size in the picture you have to get pretty close — not always recommended if the aircraft is in flight! There's no control over focusing and exposure, which seriously restricts your creativity, and the choice of films is severely limited.

Accessories are very scarce, if available at all. For example, you are generally stuck with the flash unit built into the camera, which is small and weak — fine for snapping people at parties but hopeless for lighting a Lockheed Blackbird in a dark hangar.

Finally, the image size is very small. This means that a great deal of enlargement is needed in printing to get a decent size print, which reveals all the flaws and drawbacks of the cameras and films, such as graininess, poor lens quality, and lack of film flatness. The latter is a real problem with 110 cameras. There is no way of keeping the film flat during exposure, unlike 35 mm cameras which use a pressure plate for this purpose. The natural tendency for film to

A compact camera, with its fixed wide angle lens, often tempts you into shooting when the subject is much too far away.

curl means that an image which is sharp in the centre may be slightly blurred at the edges.

COMPACT CAMERAS

Perhaps the main objection to pocket cameras is that there is now another type which incorporates the advantages of small size, lightness and ease of use while avoiding most of the drawbacks. This type is the 35 mm compact camera. These have become increasingly popular over the past few years. They take 35 mm film, like SLRs, but are as easy to use as pocket cameras — the typical model now has autofocus, automatic exposure, power film advance and built-in automatic flash. A few even have zoom lenses.

Sharp lenses, coupled with advanced focusing and exposure systems and a decent image size, give results that are often very similar to pictures taken on professional systems.

While having some of the advantages of pocket cameras, compacts also retain some of the drawbacks. With a few, not terribly impressive exceptions, they still have fixed, wide angle lenses. There is some control over focusing, but it's minimal, being restricted to locking the focus, and even that isn't available on all models. And you're still dependent on the autofocus system, which can be slow and indecisive.

Exposure control is also limited. You can play around with the film speed setting on some cameras, but the trend is for the camera to set the film speed itself, using the special DX coding pattern — a small checkerboard of black and silver squares — printed on the film cassette.

While not ideal as your first-line camera, most compacts are small enough to fit in a pocket, and so are useful when you don't want to haul around a full kit. As a visual notebook, they are perfect.

RANGEFINDER CAMERAS

The lineage of compacts can be traced back to the classic rangefinder designs. Although it uses a simple direct-vision viewfinder, the rangefinder has an optical triangulation system which makes manual focusing very accurate. You simply turn the lens focusing ring until two images in the centre of the viewfinder converge.

Once you get used to it, this system is remarkably fast and easy to use, even in dim light, where it can have the edge over an SLR. That is why you still find some press photographers using rangefinder cameras. The type also offers the kind of focusing and exposure control you get with an SLR.

The first rangefinder — indeed the first 35 mm camera of any kind — was the Leica. Other manufacturers came and went; Nikon, Canon and Contax all produced superb rangefinder models. But now the only system worth considering is the Leica.

The quality of Leica cameras is superb, but there's a high price to pay, and not just in terms of depressing your bank balance.

Although the latest models are full of mod cons, like automatic exposure, rangefinder design has generally lagged behind equivalent 35 mm SLRs. You simply don't get the same range of features, even when you're paying twice as much.

The range of lenses is also restricted compared with 35 mm systems, and they are generally available only from Leica. So for aviation work, the rangefinder is a trifle limited. For the kind of money you would have to spend on a Leica outfit, you could get a larger, and more capable, SLR kit.

SINGLE LENS REFLEX

To borrow from computer terminology, the single lens reflex camera is a WYSIWYG system — what you see is what you get. The image you see through the viewfinder is the same as the one that will eventually appear on film. The light coming through the lens is deflected by a mirror on to a focusing screen; when the button is pressed, the mirror flips out of the way, the shutter opens and the light falls on the film.

Seeing the actual image has all sorts of advantages: you know for sure if focusing is correct; you see directly the effects of different lenses, filters and so on; you can check depth of field; and metering is more precise as it, too, uses only the light which will form the final image, and is not fooled by bright or dark areas falling outside the picture frame.

SLRs come in a variety of shapes, sizes and prices, the most common being the 35 mm type. The typical camera now features at least one kind of automatic exposure, full control over shutter speed and aperture settings, automatic flash operation with dedicated flashguns, and sometimes even built-in power film advance.

Almost any feature you want can be found, from completely automatic exposure and focusing to very fast motordrives, advancing the film and firing at rates of up to six frames a second. And there's a superb choice of films to put in the camera — everything from slow, fine grain emulsions to high speed, black and white, colour negative and colour slide materials.

A full SLR kit can be expensive to build up, what with lenses, flashguns and all the other accessories. But it's money well-spent. You'll get results you simply wouldn't get any other way.

MEDIUM FORMAT AND BEYOND

Before we leave SLRs, it's worth mentioning the 35 mm type's larger cousins. Medium format SLRs, taking 120 and 220 roll film and producing image sizes of 6 x 4.5, 6 x 6, 6 x 7 and 6 x 9 cm, are commonly used by professionals and keen amateurs. Their advantage is better image quality than with 35 mm, although you usually need big enlargements before you start noticing the difference.

Medium format cameras are used for aviation work. Some are just small and light enough to be used hand-held. But the portability is nothing like as good as 35 mm SLRs, and medium format cameras are generally less sophisticated, more expensive, bulkier and slower to use than their small-film relatives. Very long lenses are either not available, or are prohibitively expensive, and very difficult to use in situations involving flying aircraft.

Depending on the exact format, and the type of film, you may get as few as ten or twelve frames per roll (double if you use 220 film in place of 120). Interchangeable film backs on cameras like the Hasselblad and Bronica systems makes it possible to change film types mid-roll, and having several backs pre-loaded speeds up film changing; but once you have to start changing the film *in* the backs, it can get dreadfully slow. Professionals who need the extra image quality — because their clients demand it or because they often make large prints — might opt for a medium format system. For most users, however, it has little to offer.

If you really want to be masochistic, you could go up another film size — and another income bracket — to large format cameras. These use cut sheet film, usually 5 x 4 inches, although 10 x 8 inches is not uncommon.

This huge image results in superbly detailed pictures, and the cameras, which can be put through an infinitely variable series of distortions, offer fabulously versatile image manipulation — which is why still life and advertizing photographers use them so much. But they demand stone-age working methods and so are agonizingly slow to use and extremely cumbersome. For all their simplicity (akin to the earliest cameras) they are also very expensive — not just to buy but to run. So large format is not even worth considering unless you are well-heeled and shooting purely static shots where your subject is prepared to keep still for a long time.

CONCLUSION

For general use, the 35 mm SLR offers the best compromise between versatility, portability and image quality. Ultimately, however, the most important thing is to use the camera that suits you. There's no point in having the finest equipment in the world if you find it awkward and complicated. That way, the equipment just gets in the way of the pictures.

CHOOSING CAMERA FEATURES

Given that the 35 mm SLR is the best type of camera for aviation work, let's assume, for a moment, that you are about to buy one. What are the features to look for?

LENS RANGE

Although all decent SLRs offer interchangeable lenses, some have a wider choice available than others. There are many different kinds of wholly incompatible lens mount, and some manufacturers have been known to produce cameras within their ranges which require special lenses. Make sure that the camera you buy has a good enough range of lenses available.

This isn't too difficult as any lenses not available in the camera manufacturer's own range can usually be obtained from independent makers. Even the more exotic items, such as the 300 mm f2.8 lens favoured by sports photographers, are now manufactured by the independents, often at prices well below those of the big name camera makers. However, it is still true that you get what you pay for, and the major professional systems camera manufacturers, such as Nikon, Canon and Pentax, have the best lenses, and the best ranges. The smaller camera manufacturers are not so well supported by independent lens makers, which is why some have adopted lens mounts found on one of the mainstream systems, particularly Pentax.

There are some additional complications here. Some cameras with special features — advanced automatic exposure modes and auto-focusing are notable examples — require lenses with special pins or fittings, or a separate range of lenses entirely. It's no use putting an ordinary lens on to an autofocus camera and expecting it to work. Check with the manufacturer, if you're in any doubt.

There are advantages to getting all your lenses from a single source, not least of which is the fact that they are all designed along the same lines. Aperture, zoom and focusing rings are in roughly the same places and, even more important, they turn in the same direction. When you're trying to photograph action subjects, you need to be able to work instinctively, and not have to look at the lens to see which way to turn the aperture ring to stop down, or which way to move the focusing to rack out to infinity. Any hesitation or fiddling around with the focusing can lose unrepeatable pictures. So it helps if there is consistency in the way the equipment works. Similarly, check the lens release and other buttons for consistent operation.

METERING SYSTEMS

It's a good idea to have a camera with automatic exposure, but which offers full manual control — or at least a decent override system. Automatic cameras are easily fooled, and aeroplanes tend to turn up in the worst possible lighting or exposure conditions, and some amount of manipulation is frequently required.

There is a lingering body of opinion which states that automatic exposure is a *bad thing* — that it implies a lack of faith in one's own abilities, or misplaced faith in the abilities of the machine. But that's unrealistic. Modern auto-exposure systems are very good. So long as you are aware of what's happening, and can help the system along when it is likely to have some trouble, there is no reason not to use it. Indeed, exposure still requires good technique, but with today's multi-mode electronic cameras the emphasis of the skills has shifted from being able to interpret the runes cast by a hand-held meter to choosing which metering and exposure system to use, and how to override it when necessary.

Automatic exposure is extremely useful, as it leaves you to concentrate on other things. With a static subject you have all the time in the world to work out your exposure. But with a moving aircraft the required exposure can change constantly as the subject moves from front-lit to side-lit to back-lit. Even with auto-exposure there are pitfalls, and it is essential to understand how your exposure system works, and what its quirks are.

Metering systems vary in the way they cover the frame. Some simply average out all the tones and give an exposure for that. It's not a bad system, although scenes with large amounts of light or dark tones will be fooled. A typical problem is the way a bright sky can lead to under-exposure of the ground. To overcome this, many exposure systems are 'centre-weighted', that is, they read the whole frame, but give slightly more importance to the centre of the picture, where your main subject is likely to be. Sometimes this weighting can be so pronounced that it almost becomes spot metering, which is where just a small fraction of the scene is metered, a system found on the Olympus OM-4 and the Nikon F4.

In recent years there has been a trend towards multi-pattern metering. Various parts of the frame are measured separately, and the distribution of tones across the frame is compared with what amounts to a computer database of typical patterns to find the right exposure. This approach makes automatic exposure more reliable in situations like back-lighting and uneven tone patterns as the system is capable of recognising these conditions.

Even multi-pattern systems can be fooled. There is no substitute for knowing about exposure and knowing how to correct it. However, the more sophisticated systems are worth having, especially in situations when you don't have the time to make complicated exposure calculations.

The type of automation also varies. The two most common types of auto-exposure are aperture priority and shutter priority. With aperture priority, you set the lens stop while the camera decides on the shutter speed. Shutter priority, of course, does it the other way around.

It's often said that using aperture priority auto-exposure is better than setting things manually because the electronic shutters on modern cameras are then capable of setting intermediate speeds between the well-known steps of 1/60th, 1/125th and so on. And that's perfectly true, although largely irrelevant. You can already get half-stops on the lens. Even if the aperture ring doesn't have actual indents at the half-stop settings, you can usually leave it set between the whole stops. And half-stop accuracy is all you need.

The labels can be misleading. For example, with an aperture priority system, you tend to spend most of your time watching the shutter speed. What happens is that you stop the lens down to something sensible and then adjust it at the time of shooting to give you the best shutter speed for the situation. You might think that you could set one shutter speed and leave it at that, but then you're not really using the system to the full. At an air show, for example, you might want 1/125th to photograph a slow-moving prop plane, to make sure you blur the propeller, and then shift to 1/500th for a fast jet.

The reason for controlling this with the aperture ring is that you want to make sure you start off with a reasonable stop. And it's easier to turn an aperture ring on the lens (which is close to the focusing ring) than to operate a dial or buttons on the top of the camera.

Aperture priority systems do have one other advantage, too. Although they need to get information from the lens about which stop is set, they don't need to have direct control over the aperture setting. The link between the camera and the lens can be simpler, and you will find that many accessories, such as close-up attachments, will work with the automatic exposure system.

So, if you have just one automatic system, aperture priority is best. Many cameras offer both systems, and more recent models come with one or more program modes too. This is where the camera sets both shutter speed and aperture. Where more than one program is offered it's because one is biased towards fast shutter speeds (for action subjects) while the other tries to give you a large depth of field with small apertures. A program mode can be useful, for when you're feeling particularly lazy or hard-pressed, but it can never be fully trusted. It's much better to have some control over what is going on.

With some cameras offering five or six exposure systems, you can spend most of your time deciding which one to use. This kind of sophistication might impress the people down at the camera club, but it doesn't really help you get better pictures. It's much better to choose one exposure system and work with it a lot — learn its foibles and find out how to correct its mistakes.

And it will make mistakes. Not one of them is perfect. That's why another feature you will want on your camera is some kind of override for the auto-exposure system. These fall into two categories:

i) Exposure compensation is usually provided by means of a ring (often linked to the film speed dial). A typical system will allow you to over- or under-expose by up to two or three stops in third-stop increments. Look for some indication in the view-finder that this is set. It's all too easy to leave it on accidentally, with the result that all your pictures are incorrectly exposed.

ii) Exposure lock is in many ways easier, and solves a problem which is most acute with centre-weighted metering systems. Imagine you are by a light-coloured concrete runway, basking in a bright sun shining down from a cloudless sky. Your camera might be telling you that a correct exposure for a general scene is something like 1/250th at $f11$. Suddenly a Harrier sporting a dark camouflage paint scheme takes up the centre of your frame. The centre-weighted exposure system takes one look at this dark mass and decides the sun has gone in and it's time to open up. If you just press the button you will end up with an exposure of, say, 1/60th at $f11$ — over-exposing the scene behind the Harrier by two stops. The aircraft itself will come out a mid-tone, which is wrong. It was dark originally and so should look dark in the picture. The simplest way round this problem is to point the camera at the general scene, hit a button to lock the exposure and then swing round to photograph the aircraft.

Exposure lock is almost essential on any camera which has a heavily centre-weighted metering system. The Nikon F3, for example, can sometimes behave as if it has semi-spot metering. Fortunately, it also has both types of exposure override, with a well-placed exposure lock button. You need to be able to press the lock button while holding the camera in the normal manner and without indulging in finger-knotting contortions.

It's also worth checking to see if the exposure stays locked all the time you keep your finger on the button. This is particularly important if you are using a motordrive. The exposure may be locked only for the first frame. The Nikon F3, mentioned above, keeps the exposure locked for all subsequent exposures — until you release the button — which is precisely what you need.

AUTOFOCUS SYSTEMS

Autofocus is becoming very popular, but it has to be used with some caution in aviation work. It can involve you in buying special lenses, and the ones you most want for aeroplane photography simply may not be available.

Why trust a machine when millions of years of evolution has provided you with a superb set of reflexes? You may be better off relying on your own reactions. If the aircraft is sitting still on the tarmac, then you have plenty of time to get the focus right. If it's moving through the air it is good betting odds that it will either be no problem for you to focus or too much of a problem for an autofocus system. Why? Well, you'll often find (depending on the length of the lens and the distance to the aircraft) that the setting you want is at, or near enough to, infinity, making fussy focusing unnecessary. Should you be using a long lens, or be fairly close to the aircraft, several things can happen with autofocus systems which make them a positive menace. It's quite possible that the shift in focus required is too rapid for the system to keep up. Changes in the lighting conditions, with unexpected bright reflections or bland areas of shadow, can confuse the system. Worst of all, just at the moment of exposure, the aircraft may move out of the centre of the frame, the small area used by the autofocus system is suddenly filled with sky, and the lens promptly racks out to infinity, leaving you with a nice shot of clouds with a blurry lump of metal in the foreground.

That's the bad news. The good news is that autofocus systems are getting better and the best ones overcome some, if not all, of the above problems. Some are even smart enough to work out the speed of the object and correct for the slight movement that occurs between the button being pressed and the shutter actually opening. Another interesting feature is the ability of some systems to lock the focus and have the shutter fire automatically when the subject is sharp. This may sound like a good idea for aeroplanes, but it makes the actual moment of taking the picture somewhat imprecise. Of course, if you find that the autofocus system isn't giving you quite what you need, you can always turn it off and focus manually, and it's nice to have the choice.

If you feel you could use some help from an autofocus system, make sure you get one which is capable of continually refocusing. Many systems focus only once for each press of the shutter button. For aviation work you really need a system which will carry on focusing the whole time the shutter button is half-depressed.

SYSTEM ACCESSORIES
Make sure the camera can accept the accessories you want — or might want in the future. You will sometimes hear professional cameras referred to as 'system' cameras. This is because they are designed to take a wide variety of additional items, from motordrives to viewfinders. The value of this adaptability has to be measured against the money you have to pay to get one of these cameras and the money you will continue to pay to add the system accessories. However, if you later find you *must* have a certain accessory, and the only way to get it is to buy a new camera, then you would have been better off getting the more expensive model in the first place.

FAST MOTORS
Perhaps the most important optional extra in aviation work is the motordrive. It is useful in several ways, not least as insurance in situations where it is difficult to get a perfect picture with a single attempt.

The classic situation is where you have an aircraft fly past you, low and fast. It requires constant refocusing, panning the camera, with one eye on possible obstacles and another on the camera systems. Even experienced photographers can turn out blurred or out-of-focus pictures under these conditions. By shooting a fast sequence, you increase your chances of one shot being sharp and properly composed. It's worth pointing out at this point that a motor is not as good as well-trained reactions. It's a truism to say that the best picture in any motordriven sequence is the one *between* two of the frames.

The best way to use a motor is to shoot when you think the picture is right, then hold down the button for a subsequent series of pictures — the insurance. Apart from anything else, it is impossible to focus the lens when the motor is firing, as the

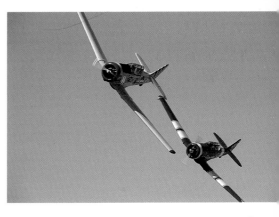

mirror spends most of its time flipping up and down. If the subject is moving towards or away from you, changing the focus to keep up with it — known as 'pulling focus' — becomes impossible. That's why you need to make your first shot the right one.

You might also want to shoot sequences for audio-visual presentations. And there are some situations where you have to use a motor to wind the film because you can't get there to do it yourself. Having strapped a camera to an aeroplane's wing, with a remote control device for triggering the shutter, it can be inconvenient to have to go out there to wind the film after each shot, especially at 5,000 feet! In fact, setting up remote control photography is often easier with a motor fitted. The camera's shutter release button is usually a mechanical device, but most motors can be triggered using a simple electrical switch, making remote firing a matter of running out a twin-strand wire with a suitable plug at the camera end and a switch at your end.

Even when you're holding the camera, a motor can make life easier, especially if you use your left eye for viewing. Having to remove the camera from your eye to wind on can break your concentration and make you miss a shot. With a motor attached, the camera is always wound on and you never have to look away from the finder.

And there is one little-discussed virtue of motordrives; they make duplicate pictures quite cheap. This is only really of interest if you are shooting on transparency film, and is of most benefit to professional photographers. Even if you have 100,000 pictures in your collection, it's always the case that two clients will want exactly the same picture at the same time. If you feel that the shot is a good one, rattling off a few extra copies with the motordrive is an inexpensive way of making high quality duplicates.

With many cameras you don't get a choice about the type of motordrive — they either won't take a motor, or they have one already built in. Having power film wind built-in is all very well, but the frame cycling usually isn't very fast. Professional photographers use cameras with motordrives that can deliver up to six frames a second, with hefty battery packs maintaining that speed for many films, which is useful when you're trying to capture a 500 mph aeroplane. Built-in motors rarely do more than two or three frames a second, and even less when the batteries start to run down.

You don't always need six frames a second, and the best type of motor allows both single frame and continuous shooting. Even better, it's handy to be able to control the continuous firing rate. Some motors allow this, many don't. Some systems, like the MD-4 motor for the Nikon F3, have an optional firing rate converter which attaches to the motor. If you don't want high speeds at all, an autowind might be a better choice than a fully-fledged motordrive. Autowinds are usually simpler and cheaper than their bigger siblings; sometimes they are single shot only, which is fine if you just want to wind to the next frame, but most now offer continuous shooting around the 1-2 frames a second mark.

One other desirable feature is power rewinding. This may seem like something of an extravagance, but in situations where things are happening thick and fast it's helpful to be able to start the film rewinding, put the camera down and carry on with another body, coming back to change the film in the first camera when there's a break in the action.

Fast motors do have one drawback, however — they eat film! With a professional system you can get through a thirty-six exposure film in as little as six seconds' continuous shooting. Not only is this expensive, it also means you tend to run out of film at critical moments. It is possible to fit 250-exposure backs to some cameras, but they are expensive, and the film can be difficult to get and even more difficult to get processed.

VIEWFINDERS

As well as strapping bits on to the bottom of the camera, professional systems also allow you to change the bit on top — the viewfinder. The vast majority of users will never need anything more than the standard prism finder which comes already bolted to the top of their cameras. However, there are a few special items around which are worth knowing about.

A few professional camera systems, notably Canon's F-1 and Nikon's F3 and F4, have interchangeable finders. Among their ranges are sports finders which make the whole frame visible when your eye is a couple of inches from the camera. As the name suggests, the large, bright image is popular among sports photographers. Aviation photographers also benefit from the ease of focusing and framing which the sports finder offers. As the finder is not pressed against the eye, spectacle wearers can see the whole frame. And there is one other benefit — the finder is easy to use even when you're wearing a helmet; the average bone dome prevents you from bringing the camera right up to your eye, and framing can often involve guesswork. With a sports finder there's no problem.

RELIABILITY

When a camera manufacturer aims a system at professionals it is putting its reputation on the line. Pros are not noted for treating their equipment with kid gloves. For that reason, professional systems are designed to be reliable — which is why they cost so much. That is good to know when *your* reputation is on the line, and the camera is out on the wing struts.

Equally, if something goes wrong, it's important to be able to get it fixed quickly. If your camera goes out during the air show season, waiting six weeks for it to be fixed could mean missing half a dozen important shows. Independent camera repairers can sometimes offer a quick turn-round, but usually only on the more popular professional systems. And the people who make those systems usually provide fast servicing, and not just for professionals — although you may have to live near a major city to reap the benefit.

31

HIRING ACCESSORIES

The last major benefit of using a professional system is that it is much easier to hire lenses and accessories — and sometimes borrow equipment from the manufacturer. Most of the big names, Nikon, Canon, Olympus and Pentax, operate loan schemes, although they usually insist on proof that you are a professional.

If you really need a special lens or camera, can't borrow it and can't raise the mortgage to buy it, it may be possible to hire it. Again this will necessitate a trip to a big city, if you're not already there, but it's worth it. Hire rates can be surprisingly low, although there is usually a hefty deposit required if you're not paying by credit card. But don't expect to find an underwater fisheye lens for your rare Itchikura 2000 — it's strictly mainstream systems in these places.

OTHER TYPES

Even when you're buying something other than a 35 mm SLR, many of these points still apply. The rule is to go for the maximum flexibility, even if you don't think you'll need it straight away. For example, if you plan to get a compact camera, perhaps as a notebook or back-up camera, be wary of those which set the film speed themselves, using the DX coding on the film cassette. The film speed setting is usually the only method you have of overriding the auto-exposure system. Admittedly, you're probably buying a compact precisely because you don't want to think about things like that. However, you never know when you might want to be clever.

Check how many steps the autofocus system uses. Focusing is rarely a continuous process. Instead, the camera uses a number of discrete steps, very much along the lines of the head-and-shoulders, group and mountain symbols found on very simple cameras. Depth of field compensates for any slight lack of accuracy. The fewer the steps, the more you are relying on depth of field and the greater chance you have of less than absolutely crisp results. Three steps is a little crude, twenty is overkill — a good compromise is around seven or eight. Finally, telephoto attachments are best avoided, although those that come built-in are usable.

THE LENS

More than anything, your collection of lenses dictates the kind of pictures you are going to get. When you bought your SLR camera, it is likely that it came with a lens. At one time this would invariably have been a 50 mm 'standard', but now could just as easily be a short-range zoom — perhaps a 35-70 mm. If you stick with just this one lens you will find the type of pictures you can attempt very limited. In particular, shots of flying aircraft are likely to end up as insignificant dots in acres of empty sky.

Other lenses, with longer or shorter focal lengths, are needed to help you close in on distant action, or fit all of a large and close object into the frame. But before we look at the subject of focal length, let's consider another characteristic of the ideal aviation photographer's lens — speed.

SPEED

You will often find that there are several versions of a particular focal length, even within a single manufacturer's range. The difference between the models is their 'speed' — that is, the size of their maximum apertures. The longer the lens, the less speed it tends to have. For example, a common 50 mm lens has a maximum aperture of $f1.8$, but a typical speed for a 300 mm lens is $f4$. However, 300 mm lenses with wider maximum apertures are available. These 'faster' lenses typically have a maximum aperture of $f2.8$.

There are two main reasons why you might want this extra speed. The first is fairly obvious — low light. When the scene starts to get dark, having a fast lens can allow you to open up further and carry on taking photographs without resorting to long exposure times (and a tripod), or strapping on a flashgun.

Fast lenses, such as this 300 mm $f2.8$, give snappy focusing and a bright viewfinder image. But they are large, heavy and very expensive

The other reason — less obvious but actually more relevant to the aviation photographer — is that faster lenses are easier to focus. For a start, the image in the viewfinder, which is formed with the lens at its maximum aperture, is brighter. In addition, the depth of field — the area in front of and behind the main subject which is also sharp — in the viewing image is much shallower, focusing errors are not so well hidden and the picture tends to snap in and out of focus much more clearly and decisively.

Another, incidental, reason is for people who might want to use a teleconverter, an optical device which effectively boosts the focal length of a lens. As we will see, adding a teleconverter results in some loss of speed. If you are using a slow lens to start with, this can be quite serious, so it is better to start off with a fast lens.

How useful are these benefits? Well, there may be times when you need some more speed to get a reasonable exposure. However, most aviation pictures are shot in reasonable light, with the lens stopped down to give good depth of field and to get the maximum quality out of the optics — lenses always give their best performance a few stops down from the maximum.

The improved focusing, on the other hand, can be invaluable, especially with telephotos from 200 mm and up, where focusing tends to be more critical anyway — wide angles tend to have so much depth of field that small errors are often covered up.

As usual, there is a catch. Faster lenses are invariably more expensive, sometimes horrifically so. And by their very nature they are more bulky. This can have repercussions beyond taking up camera-bag space and using more of your energy to lug them around. For instance, a 200 mm with a normal maximum aperture of, say, $f3.5$ may well have the same size front element as your other, shorter lenses. That means it can take the same filters. A faster lens, because it has to gather more light, will have a larger front element, and you may have to buy a separate set of filters for it. Some fast lenses can become so large that filters are fitted into special slots at the rear of the lens.

Those problems aside, it is a wise choice to go for the faster lens whenever you have the option, and can afford it. It's worth noting that speed is one area where zoom lenses lose out. The complicated optics of zooms make it difficult to build fast versions without the quality suffering. This is a good reason for sticking to fixed-length telephoto lenses, although zooms are handy at shorter lengths where speed isn't so crucial.

Shooting moving aircraft, particularly head-on, requires rapid and constant refocusing. This is where a fast lens, with its snappy focusing and bright image, is useful

FOCAL LENGTH

Although you automatically think of long lenses when it comes to photographing aeroplanes, there's no hard and fast rule. Wide angles can be used for pictures of airborne aircraft (especially if you are airborne at the same time), while telephotos are often useful for static shots, especially for getting details when you can't get past a barrier or through a fence. So the following guidelines are just that — rules to be broken as often as possible.

You really need a wide range of focal lengths to photograph aircraft. You need telephotos to pull in the action when the aircraft is far away, and you need wide angles for when you get close.

The standard 50 mm lens, so often bought with the camera, is a reasonable all-rounder for general photographic subjects, but it falls into the 'neither one thing nor the other' category when it comes to aviation work.

TELEPHOTOS

A lot of your time is likely to be spent taking pictures of airborne aeroplanes performing flypasts or displays. With a standard lens, the subject will look like a dot in the picture, even when it seems reasonably large in the viewfinder. You need a lens which produces a larger image, which is where telephotos come in.

It's worth pausing to explain what is meant by a 'telephoto', as the term is sometimes misunderstood. The focal length of a simple one-element lens is the distance from the lens to the point where light coming from infinity is focused. The longer this distance, the bigger the image formed by the lens, so a 200 mm lens produces an image twice the size of that given by a 100 mm lens.

This would be fine until you start getting up to lengths like 500 mm. With a conventional design, the photographic lens would have to be at least 500 mm long. Fortunately, there is a way around

Usefulness of long lenses: when you're restricted to the crowd line, a medium telephoto like an 85 mm is often not quite long enough, although if you use the ground well, as in this shot, the results can be perfectly adequate. Switching to a longer lens, in this case a 180 mm, pulls in the subject this. Telephoto designs, as distinct from conventional 'long focus' lenses, use special combinations of elements to produce lenses which are physically shorter than their effective focal lengths. (The opposite of this approach is known as 'retrofocus', and is commonly used in wide angle lenses to give sufficient clearance between the rear of the lens and the film for the camera's mirror and shutter mechanisms.)

Snapping a telephoto lens on to the front of your camera is a little like shooting through a telescope, with the same pros and cons. You certainly 'get closer' to the subject without doing any footwork, and a long lens can often be the only way of getting the shot. But there are penalties. The lens is bigger and heavier than the standard, and like a telescope, small amounts of camera shake or vibration are magnified. The really long lenses can be expensive, too.

Nevertheless, some kind of long lens is essential kit. Much of the time your prey will be far away, either because it is airborne or because you are at a location where photography is permitted but movement is restricted, such as an airport. Airshows tend to be a combination of both. So what kind of long lens do you want?

Those amateur photographers able to resist the lure of zooms often choose a 135 mm as their first — and often only — telephoto. And this isn't a bad choice for general photography and even some aviation work. Add one really long lens to this and you could do almost anything. However, if you intend to purchase a full range of lenses eventually, you will find that the 135 mm becomes redundant as you buy more useful lenses which straddle this length.

A short telephoto, around 85 mm or 100 mm, is an excellent general purpose lens. You will be able to shoot aircraft on the ramp, details of static aircraft and portraits of pilots — assuming you can get close enough. It is also quite useful for shooting formations and air-to-air work, particularly if you can avoid photographing through glass.

A 200 mm lens allows you to start photographing flying aeroplanes from the crowd line, especially large aircraft and small formation displays. And it is still flexible enough to allow hand-held shots of static displays and people.

For the best ground-to-air shots, however, you need to bring in the big artillery. A 300 mm or 400 mm lens is an essential part of any aviation photographer's kit. The choice between those two lengths is up to you. Certainly, the 400 mm gives you an edge, but it is heavier and more prone to emphasizing camera shake.

You can go even longer — 500 mm or 600 mm — but at about this point you hit a law of diminishing returns. Longer lenses will allow you to close in tighter on distant aircraft. But the lenses are more difficult to use and reduce your chances of getting sharp pictures. Apart from the camera shake problems, the angle, or field of view, through very long lenses is so small that it is difficult to keep up with fast-moving subjects. Most people have had the experience of seeing something and then being unable to find it through binoculars because they are looking at such a small part of the scene. Very long lenses create this sort of problem all the time, although it diminishes the more you use the lens.

One system that attempts to solve at least some of the problems is the mirror lens. This is a cunning device closely related to astronomical telescopes. The earliest such devices, dating from the seventeenth century, used a large concave mirror which focused the light on to another mirror which in turn reflected it into the eye of the astronomer. This is known as a 'catoptric' system. Later designs added conventional lens elements, and are known as 'catadioptic' systems, which is why you sometimes hear of mirror lenses based on this idea referred to as 'cats'.

The light path in a mirror lens is effectively 'folded'. Light coming in at the front hits a mirror at the back and is reflected on to a small mirror set into the centre of the front element. This mirror reflects the light through lens elements set into the centre of the main mirror which finally focus the image in the camera. This back-and-forth shuttling of the light path means that a lens can have a focal length of, say, 500 mm while being only 150 mm long. And it has one unique effect: points of light rendered out of focus in the image show up as rings, or 'doughnuts' of light, instead of blurred discs.

As usual there are drawbacks. With very rare exceptions, mirror lenses are incapable of having the same kind of aperture controls as normal lenses and so most have none at all — the maximum aperture of the lens is the only one you get. Normally this isn't too bad — $f5.6$ is not uncommon for a 500 mm mirror lens. But if you want to stop down, you can't. When the light gets too bright you have to add neutral density filters. As depth of field is an important consideration in aviation work, this point alone makes mirror lenses a dubious choice. The final nails in the coffin are that mirrors are rarely as sharp as their conventional equivalents, are susceptible to damage and make filtering difficult, often taking special rear-mounted filters.

The news is slightly better when it comes to teleconverters. These are devices which sit between the lens and the camera, effectively increasing the focal length. A typical teleconverter will boost the focal length by 1.4x, so that a 200 mm becomes a 280 mm. Converters which double the focal length are also common.

In most cases, having a converter stuck on the back was not something the designer originally considered when calculating the optimum configuration for the lens. So teleconverters can result in some loss of image quality. And they always result in some loss of speed. A lens with a maximum aperature of, say, $f2.8$ will have an effective maximum aperture of $f4$ once a 2x converter is fitted. This means you have a lower low-light capability and the image in the viewfinder is darker. And a converter is slower to fit than a conventional lens.

Balanced against these drawbacks is the fact that you can effectively gain a new range of lenses at minimal cost. Because they don't have aperture or focusing mechanisms — those are still handled by the main lens — teleconverters can be quite cheap. If you can't decide between buying a 300 mm or a 400 mm lens, you could buy the 300 mm and a 1.4x converter and have both!

To avoid problems with poor image quality, it's a good idea to go for the more expensive converters. Undoubtedly the best are those designed specifically for a small range of lenses — for example, Nikon produces a converter just for its fast telephoto lenses. And it's worth noting that you can't use converters on just any lens. Apart from dedicated units designed to work with just one lens or range of lenses, most converters are intended for telephotos. The average telephoto is quite a simple design. Wide angle lenses, on the other hand, are complex designs which a converter will only upset. Used with care and discretion, however, a good teleconverter is a valuable asset.

WIDE ANGLES

If telephoto lenses are like using a telescope, then wide angles are like looking through the wrong end of that telescope. However, their main effect is not just to make objects seem further away, but to include more of the scene in the shot.

Wide angle lenses are said to have a wider 'angle of view'. If you imagine a pyramid, with its tip at the lens, extending along the line of sight. Its sides are defined by the edges of the frame. The angle of view is the angle between the sides, at the tip of the pyramid. With a 50 mm lens this is forty-six degrees, but narrows to a little over eight degrees when you get up to a 300 mm lens. Wide angle lenses expand the angle of view. A 24 mm lens has a viewing angle of eighty-four degrees.

The most common wide angle lenses, in ascending angle of view, are the 35 mm, 28 mm and 24 mm. Beyond that you get into the realm of the ultra-wide lens, with focal lengths of 20 mm, 18 mm and even as wide as 13 mm. And there are lenses beyond that, known as 'fisheyes' which typically have angles of view of 180 degrees, although Nikon has one with a viewing angle of 220 degrees, so that it actually looks slightly behind itself!

The most common fault with wide angle lenses is their tendency towards 'barrel distortion'. This is where straight lines in the subject are seen to bow outwards in the image, the effect being most pronounced near the edges of the frame. Telephotos are prone to a similar distortion, known as 'pincushion', where the lines bow inwards. You can run a quick and dirty check for this kind of problem by lining up a straight edge — say a doorframe — along the edge of the frame. If the edge does not run smoothly along the frame boundary, then barrel distortion is present.

Lens manufacturers attempt to correct this distortion using special lens elements. The result is that progressively wider lenses get progressively more complex, expensive and slower. With fisheye lenses, however, they give up and let barrel distortion have free rein, which is why these lenses have their uniquely distorted style.

Fisheye lenses fall into two groups. Some are called 'full-frame' in that they still cover the whole picture area. Others form a circular image within the frame, and so are known — not surprisingly — as circular fisheyes.

Given their extreme cost, it is perhaps fortunate that fisheye lenses have very limited applications in aviation photography. You may be able to get some interesting cockpit shots with them, and they have been used occasionally for pictures of an aircraft from a camera strapped to a wing, tail or strut. But on the whole, the distortion is often unsympathetic, frequently distracts from the picture's interest and is usually tediously predictable. So fisheyes are things to be used infrequently, and with discretion. If you want to experiment with one you're better off hiring it for a couple of days. On the other hand, normal wide angle lenses are very useful, and one or two examples should be in every aviation photographer's kitbag.

As the biggest problem in photographing flying aircraft is in getting a large enough image of the subject, wide angle lenses are not an obviously essential item for the aviation photographer. Yet there are some occasions when you can't help but get close to the subject. Wide angles have all kinds of advantages which include the ability to take shots of aircraft in the cramped conditions you might find in hangars and museums and the ability to get closer to static aircraft, and thus put the rest of the crowd behind you. This is especially useful for photographing close-up details of aircraft. A wide angle lens is often the only way of getting a shot inside a small cockpit — to get the person alongside you in a Cessna, a 24 mm or wider is essential. Cockpits are not known for their generous elbow room, and even with a 35 mm you can wind up with nothing more than the pilot's ear, unless you are prepared to shoot from outside the cabin (not recommended at heights of anything more than zero feet).

You may even want to use a wide angle for some types of flying shots. If the aircraft is going to come close, and you want

Very wide angle lenses distort the shape of aircraft by making you get close to the subject. A 24 mm wide angle was used on this AV-8B showing that the distortion can be used to good effect

to give an impression of how low it is, a wide angle lens will allow you to include some ground detail. Or you might want to get a broad shot of an airfield or group of aircraft, and pictures of people with aircraft, all of which require a more sweeping angle of view. Finally, these lenses are less susceptible to camera shake, which makes them useful for air-to-air work.

Just as the 135 mm is often the first telephoto, so the 35 mm is frequently the first wide angle of the amateur photographer. In this case, however, this is no bad thing. Many people find themselves using the 35 mm in place of the 'standard' 50 mm. Indeed, fixed-lens compact cameras usually have lenses of around this focal length.

The 35 mm is a good choice for shots of aircraft on the ground. It gives you a reasonably wide view, so you don't have to stand back too far, while avoiding the distortion invited by wider lenses.

At least one even wider lens is a good idea for cockpit interiors and static shots of large aircraft, and for the more advanced kinds of remote control photography. The best all-rounder here is the 24 mm. A 20 mm or 21 mm can come in handy occasionally, but for most people probably won't earn its keep.

If you don't want to buy more than one wide angle lens, then a 28 mm is a good compromise in place of separate 35 mm and 24 mm lenses, and some may find it a better first choice than the 35 mm, although you may not find it wide enough for the cramped conditions of some cockpits.

ZOOMS

Having a wide range of lenses does lead to one problem — you have to keep changing them all the time. It is axiomatic that the lens you have on the camera at any one time is always precisely the *wrong* one. Having more than one camera body alleviates this somewhat, but you can still spend a lot of time changing lenses. When there's a lot going on at a busy air show, that can mean missed shots.

A zoom lens, which covers a range of focal lengths is an obvious solution. You can change the focal length in a split second. Furthermore, you can choose 'in between' lengths — you don't have to choose between 85 mm or 200 mm; you can have 125 mm, 157 mm and anything else if you like. Of course, a zoom doesn't give you an unlimited choice of lengths. Each zoom has a defined range — 70-210 mm for example. But as lens designs get better, these ranges are getting bigger all the time.

There is a danger with zooms, in that they can make you lazy. It is too easy to zoom the lens to fine-tune the composition rather than changing your position. As the perspective of the final image is determined by your position relative to the subject, and not by the focal length, this can lead to pictures which are well-framed but which could have been greatly improved by zooming the photographer rather than the lens! Zooms can also slow you down. It is tempting to spend too much time fiddling with fine adjustments of the focal length setting and wind up missing the shot — or having it out of focus because you didn't have time to do that as well.

Due mainly to the complexity of their design, zooms have slower maximum apertures than conventional lenses (although this situation is slowly improving), especially at the longer focal length, and the speed may vary as the lens is zoomed. And they are inherently bulky and heavy.

However, if you are stuck in one position, a zoom might be crucial. In air-to-air photography, for example, it is difficult to walk up to the subject, and changing lenses in the cramped confines of a cockpit can be an unrewarding experience.

There remains a stigma about zoom lenses. It is still felt by many people that zooms do not have the sharpness of fixed

In the cramped confines of a cockpit, a wide angle is essential as you can't step back to get more in. A 15 mm wide angle was used for this shot of an HH-46 Sea Knight flight deck

length lenses. And there is at least a partial basis for this belief. Zooms are complicated beasts which make it more difficult for the lens designer to come up with a combination of elements which can correct for all distortions and aberrations at all focal lengths. A zoom which is perfect at its shortest setting may suffer distortion at the other end of the range. The problem is most acute with zooms which start off in the wide angle region and go up into the telephoto area. Wide angle and telephoto lenses have different problems which require different solutions from the lens designer. A zoom which spans both regions can only ever be a compromise. And the same is true for zooms which cover huge ranges.

The solution to this problem is to throw money at it. Get the best quality lens you can afford — and that's true whether you're buying zooms or conventional lenses. And don't go for over-ambitious zooms. Stick to those which cover short, but useful ranges: 70–210 mm and 35–70 mm are good choices. Some people like 100–300 mm zooms, but by the time you are getting to focal lengths that long, you will probably want more speed than a zoom can offer. By sticking to shorter, more modest, zooms, as well as ensuring image quality, you will suffer less from the poor maximum apertures which most zooms have.

One-touch zooms are generally better for aviation work than two-touch models. The one-touch lens uses the same ring for both focusing and zooming. You twist the ring in the normal method to focus, and push or pull it to zoom. A two-touch lens uses separate rings for the two functions, and is invariably slower to use. The only advantage of the two-touch is that you can focus the image at the maximum focal length — focusing is always easier the longer the lens — and then zoom out to the required length for shooting. This only applies if the lens is a true zoom, as opposed to a varifocal lens which doesn't maintain focus as the focal length is changed; but most lenses these days *are* true zooms. It is difficult to maintain focus while zooming with a one-touch. However, for aviation work, speed of operation is far more important.

LENS FEATURES

When choosing a lens, there are a few things to look for, and the first is the price tag. Whatever lenses you get, there is something they should all have — quality. Go for the best you can afford. There is little point in spending a fortune on a camera only to pinch pennies with the lens. Cameras systems are like hi-fi systems — the most important bit is the one at the sharp end. In a hi-fi, the crucial element is the one which produces the signal — the cartridge, laser or tape head. Without a good signal, there is nothing the amplifier or speakers can do to put things right. The same is true with a camera system. If your lens has the optical quality of a milk bottle, you might as well throw away your expensive camera and use a box with a hole cut in it. But if you start with a crisp image, the rest is easy.

Next, take a look at the focusing action. It needs to be smooth and quite light. When you're trying to catch moving aircraft, it's important to be able to focus quickly and confidently. For the same reason, the focusing action should work in the same direction on all your lenses, and the same goes for the aperture ring.

There are two special types of focusing worth considering — both found on long telephotos. The first, and most common, is internal focusing. Unlike most lenses, which rack out all or most of the elements, moving them further away from the film to focus on closer objects, internal focusing moves just a few elements, buried inside the lens. That means you are moving less glass and metal around, and the lens always stays the same size. The result is fast and smooth focusing and better handling generally. The quality also tends to be better, as it is easier to produce a design which gets rid of optical aberrations this way.

The other system is follow-focus. These lenses, pioneered by the Novoflex company, use a pistol-like grip which is squeezed to focus. It takes some getting used to, but can be very effective. However, you still have to develop normal focusing skills for your other lenses, and you might fight it hard to justify the inevitably high cost of these special optics.

The other major consideration is the filter size. You don't want to have to buy a separate set of filters for each lens. Getting lenses which share the same filter size — or, at the most, two sizes, will save you money. Stepping rings, which screw into the lens and accept filters of a different size, can help, but can complicate matters when it comes to fitting lens hoods.

While on the subject of lens hoods, when aircraft — or photographers — are flying round the sky, it is tricky to anticipate where the sun will be coming from in relation to your subject. It is difficult to arrange the subject so that the sun is always over your shoulder: nor would it be entirely desirable, as it would lead to dull and predictable shots.

So, you are likely to be faced with the problem of taking shots into or near the sun. Strong points of light, such as the sun, lead to stray light bouncing around inside the lens, causing an effect known as 'flare'. This can manifest itself either as an overall lowering of contrast or as blobs of light, which often take on the shape of the lens aperture.

This problem can be greatly reduced by using a lens hood or shade. The simplest version is a tube which screws into the filter mount of the lens (or the filter itself if fitted). It's important to get the right hood for the lens. A hood designed for, say, a 200 mm lens will be quite long and narrow, to make it as effective as possible. But fit that to a 24 mm and you will have real problems. The wider angle of view of the shorter lens will be restricted by the hood, so that the edges of the picture will be cut off.

Metal hoods are usually better than the rubber variety. Rubber hoods are forever collapsing at the wrong moment. And a metal lens hood also provides some protection for the lens. Should you bump the front of the lens against the canopy or fuselage during a spot of turbulence, the hood will soak up the blow to some extent and avoid getting scratches on the lens surface.

The longer telephoto lenses frequently have built-in hoods which slide forward when required. The problem with these is that they often slide backwards again without warning. If the hood has no mechanism for locking it in place, a piece of sticky tape ('gaffer' tape is best) will hold it in position.

FILM CHOICE

Film is where photographic technology has made its greatest advances over the past decade. Speed and resolution — normally conflicting attributes — have both improved dramatically. And this has led to photographers being faced with a bewildering choice of films. Yet using the right film is as important to getting optimum results as choosing the right lens.

The precise brands and products available to you depend on where you are in the world. And films are always being introduced — or abandoned. However, we can look at the qualities you need for aviation work — with reference to a few of the old faithfuls — so that you know what to look for when you try out a film.

The most immediate consideration is speed. The sensitivity of film to light varies — the more sensitive films are said to be faster. The speed of a film is indicated by a number, calibrated in either ASA or DIN units. The system introduced by the American Standards Association (ASA), and since adopted internationally as the ISO standard, is the more common and is the one we'll use here, although the slightly earlier Deutsche Industrie Norm (DIN) system is still used widely in Europe. In both cases, the higher the number, the faster the film.

ISO values work in a similar way to shutter speeds, in that a doubling of the number represents one stop: ISO 100 is twice as fast as ISO 50 and so is one stop faster, while ISO 200 and 400 are two and three stops faster, being four and eight times the speed.

Having a more sensitive film means you can use a shorter exposure time or a smaller stop — or a combination of the two. As we will see later, these are both worthwhile features for the aviation photographer, so you would assume that the best film for this kind of work is the fastest you can possibly get. Not so.

As a rule, films are made faster by having an emulsion — the light-sensitive coating — with larger grains of the light-sensitive chemicals, known as halides. The larger the grain, the sooner it is affected by light. The problem is that, as a result of the exposure and development process, these grains tend to clump together, and the clumps can be visible in the picture (you need a microscope to see the individual grains, although the clumping is confusingly referred to as the 'grain' of the image). The effect is more pronounced with the larger grains you find in fast film.

Interestingly, slide films suffer less from graininess for a very simple reason. With all films, the initial exposure creates what is known as a 'latent' image: the emulsion has been chemically altered by exposure to light but the effect — that of exposed grains turning black — is not great enough to be visible. In the development process, the original effect is amplified using chemicals to produce the visible, negative image. Naturally, this image will tend to be composed of the larger grains, as they are the first to be affected. With a negative, that's the only image you've got. With a slide film, however, the film is re-exposed to light or treated chemically, to create the final, positive image, and the original picture is bleached away. This means the final image is composed of the smaller, slower grains which were not sufficiently affected by the in-camera exposure to show up at the negative stage.

If you use films of ISO 100 or slower, and especially if the pictures are rarely enlarged above 10 x 8 inches, grain will be hardly, if at all, noticeable. With faster films, particularly of ISO 400 or more, grain can be very intrusive. Even if — as is sometimes the case — it looks attractive, this graininess does result in loss of detail and sharpness. In aviation work, you often need to enlarge a picture because you couldn't get close enough, or use a long enough lens, to make the subject a decent size in the frame. If you use fast film, the results can be dreadful.

So you need to strike a balance between high film speed, for coping with fast subjects or low light, and slow emulsions for detail.

CONFLICT DIAGRAM

S	F		depth of field	$\rightarrow$	F	F
L	I	$\leftarrow$	*big enlargements*		A	I
O	L		fast shutter speed	$\rightarrow$	S	L
W	M	$\leftarrow$	*fine detail*		T	M

There are three main film media — colour slides, colour negatives (for prints) and black and white negatives. It is largely a matter of personal preference which you use, although if you want to sell your pictures for reproduction it is usually better to shoot colour transparencies. They can always be converted to monochrome if that is what the editor of the magazine or book needs. And for technical reasons, colour transparencies reproduce better than prints. If you plan to sell prints, on the other hand, shooting on colour or mono negative makes printing easier and cheaper.

Monochrome photography is becoming a neglected art, now that shooting in colour is so easy. Black and white pictures, when done properly, do have a unique beauty. And to get the most out of those qualities you have to shoot in black and white from the start — converting from colour at a later stage is fine for reproduction, but never gives sufficient quality for really top class prints.

Black and white film is still more forgiving with wrong or difficult exposures, which is why some people abuse it. And the same goes for colour negative film. Negative films are said to have more 'latitude' than transparency materials, which is generally thought to mean you can get away with bad exposures. But to get a top quality image, negative films have to be exposed and processed just as carefully as colour transparencies.

However, shooting on negative film does give you more room for manipulation and fun, in that you can print your own pictures with a comparatively small investment in equipment and materials. Colour printing can be expensive and

:

difficult, but black and white printing is very easy — and enjoyable.

Printing is an additional creative step in the photographic process. Skilled printers can turn an average picture into something quite stunning through manipulation of the tonal values, colours, contrast, framing and even the aspect ratio of the shot — the relative sizes of the width and height of the print. And it is sometimes possible to rescue a shot which suffered a disaster at the shooting stage, although it's best not to rely on this.

As well as just printing the picture, you can apply a variety of special processes. For example, colour toning can be used to good effect on mono prints. Although, like any special effect, it has to be used with taste and restraint, colour toning can add to the mood of a picture. The most obvious, and cliched, example is to use sepia toning to give a nostalgic feel to shots of vintage aircraft. Something like blue or green tints on shots of modern jets is less corny, and can be more graphic, especially if the print is generally quite dark. A subtle nuance of colour is far more attractive than something that pokes you in the eyeballs. Toning kits are widely available, and the processes are usually fairly simple.

Other processes, such as texture screens and special effects, are available, but need to be used with extreme caution. They often take over the picture, and in any case are rarely appropriate to a subject like aeroplanes.

Black and white film is also capable of being 'pushed' more easily. If you find yourself in a situation where the film is just too slow, it is possible to uprate it — that is, give it a higher ISO rating. You might, for example, rate an ISO 400 film at ISO 800 or even ISO 1600, making it one or two stops faster. That in turn allows you to use a faster shutter speed to cut down camera shake or subject blur or a smaller stop for more depth of field. What you are doing, in effect, is underexposing the film, and to make up for this the film has to be pushed at the processing stage, usually by giving it more time in the developer. As you have to process the whole film at one, you can't uprate the film for individual shots — it has to be done for the whole roll.

Getting the processing right does take some experimentation, and there are penalties; more graininess and higher contrast being the most common. Many colour films do not respond well to being pushed and make their protest known by giving the shots a colour cast. But there are fewer problems with monochrome film, and pushing can be a useful option when the light dies on you.

As we have seen, the only real drawback to shooting in black and white is that it limits the market for your pictures, as most magazine and book editors want colour. Of course, that might not worry you.

If you want to shoot in colour, you have to make a decision about how you want to use the pictures. If they are destined for an album or a wall, then you will want to shoot on negative film in order to get prints.

On the other hand, if you are shooting for reproduction, or you are simply not sure where the pictures will end up, you should probably think about using transparency film. As well as being the best bet for selling pictures, transparencies also offer you the possibility of projecting your pictures — even producing complete audio-visual presentations. Also, these days you can produce extremely high-quality prints directly from slides, albeit at a higher price than printing from negatives. Going the other way — producing a slide from a negative — is more difficult and results in some loss of quality.

Without the option to correct things at the printing stage, the choice of colour transparency material — the make and type of film — has a profound and direct effect on the final image. For example, different films have different colour bias. Some are said to be warmer than others, or they have better greens, or whatever. Contrast, and the ability of films to handle shadow detail, also varies. That kind of thing is entirely down to personal preference, and you really need to try a wide variety of films to find the one you like. Even if you think you are already using the perfect film, it's worth sampling others, especially new materials which come on to the market.

There are a few points to bear in mind when you test a film you've never used before. For a start, think about the kind of conditions you are shooting under. If you take shots outside on a dull, overcast day, don't be surprised if the colour is a little on the blue side. Ideally, you would shoot a test card, which has carefully controlled 'standard' colours on it. And you would do it under standard lighting conditions. But few people could, or would want to, set up that kind of thing. In any case, pictures of test cards don't really give you a good 'feel' for the film's characteristics.

A better method is to shoot a roll of your favourite film alongside the new one. Although hardly a scientific test, this at least allows you to make subjective comparisons: is the new film warmer in colour, does it have more contrast or grain?

If you can, it's worth getting professional films, although they have to be looked after. After leaving the factory, film continues to 'ripen', eventually reaching its optimum speed and colour accuracy. Then, after a while, it starts to go off, losing that speed and becoming prone to colour casts, which is why films have use-by dates on them.

Amateur films, which might sit on the dealer's shelf and in the user's camera for a long time, ripen and decay slowly, and are fairly robust. Professional films, which are likely to be used within weeks, days or even hours of being bought, are practically at their best when they leave the factory, and start to go off sooner. So why use them? Well, they tend to be sharper, have finer grain and better colour than amateur films. The price for this extra quality is that they need to be kept cool when not in use. Most professionals have a fridge just for the film — taking them out at least an hour before shooting to let them warm up, and avoid condensation problems. Keeping the film in the shade, or one of those 'cooler' bags is recommended once you're out and about. In fact, that sort of treatment would not be amiss with amateur films too.

You should also think about how long you want the pictures to last *after* you have shot and processed them. No image lasts for ever: the chemical structure of the image slowly breaks down and the image fades, even if you keep it in the dark. This happens to slides and negatives as much as prints.

With monochrome pictures, you slowly lose the image. With colour it's worse, as the three colour layers which make up the image fade at different rates. The result is that, even before you see a loss of density, the picture takes on a colour cast. You only have to look at colour pictures shot in the 1950s to see how unattractive this can be.

As well as thinking about preserving your own memories, professional photographers selling stock pictures need to have images which will stick around for a while to earn their keep. The good news is that film stocks are getting better all the time. The bad news is that longevity varies enormously according to the quality of the processing, which is often out of your hands. However, there are some things you can do to help.

Colour negative materials are the least stable. A poorly processed negative might last for only five years before showing some deterioration. Colour transparencies are by far the best with Kodachrome way ahead at the top of the scale. Kodak claim that a well-stored Kodachrome will last in excess of 100 years. This is why pictures shot for library and archive purposes are often on Kodachrome.

One of the reasons Kodachrome is so good in this respect is that Kodak controls the processing itself. If you use other materials, choose a processor with a good reputation — perhaps one that professionals use.

Careful storage of the negatives and transparencies is a great help, too: you don't have to worry so much about prints because, if you have the negatives, you can always print some more.

High humidity and temperature are the worst enemies of photographic materials. The lower the temperature the better. Some people deep-freeze their most important negatives, as storing them at temperatures of $-10°C$ to $-20°C$ can increase the longevity by a factor of between 100 and 1,000.

On a simpler scale, careful selection of storage materials can help. Acid-free archive boxes and transparency sleeves are available — some plastic storage sleeves intended for transparencies actually accelerate the dye-fading process as they react chemically with the film. And if you have a negative which you use very frequently, or you intend to use it for a long run of prints, it might be worth having a high-quality duplicate made and using that instead. The same goes for transparencies used for projection. Every time you shine the bright light of an enlarger or projector on an image it fades a little more.

So what are the best films? For colour transparencies, a speed of ISO 50 or 64 is fast enough for most aviation work, as you are usually outdoors, and it will give you extremely sharp results. If you need a little extra speed, perhaps to avoid camera shake with long lenses, ISO 100 materials still retain excellent sharpness while giving you another stop. And this speed is also a good starting point for negative materials. You can switch to ISO 200 when the light starts to go, or for some indoor work. And in dim light, where you can't use a tripod or flash, ISO 400 and faster films can prove useful, but you do start to suffer from loss of sharpness through increased grain.

Once you've made your initial investment in equipment, film is likely to be the main cost, and it can prove very expensive, so it's worth looking after. Keep it in a cool place and get it processed soon after exposing it.

Finally, of all the items you might spend your hard-earned money on, film is perhaps the most important. Once you have a reasonable hardware outfit, you are better off buying film rather than getting yet another lens or filter. It is practice that will make you a better photographer, and will also help you define exactly what other items of kit you might need — if any.

FILTERS

The best filters for aviation work are discussed in the technique section, but there are a few useful points to bear in mind when buying.

For a start, it is essential to use good quality filters. There is simply no point in spending vast amounts of money on lenses if you're going to stick something with truly dreadful optical qualities in front of them. However, that does not necessarily mean buying the most expensive. There are many excellent brands at reasonable prices.

There are two basic systems — the type that screw into the front of the lens, and the type that slot into a special carrier (which screws into the front of the lens). Both have their advantages and drawbacks.

The slot-in variety are certainly faster to change, and make possible various special types, in particular graduated filters. To get the full benefit, however, you really need a separate holder on each lens, otherwise you will be slowed down considerably changing the holder with every change of lens. Fortunately, the holders are rarely that expensive. One real drawback is the difficulty of providing adequate lens shielding. With a conventional filter, a lens hood can be screwed on to the filter itself. Most slot-in filter systems do provide lens hoods, but they are usually woefully inadequate. In studios, where the filter concept originated, this was not a problem. Lenses could be shielded in other ways, if necessary. With aeroplanes, however, you are usually out in the open, aiming the camera at the sky, and inviting the sun to shine into the edge of the filter, producing flare, cutting down contrast, and generally making life difficult. A good lens hood is an essential item on every lens.

Conventional filters are generally less problematic, especially for action work. Although slow to change, the problem can be minimized by buying a few extra filters, so that each lens has its own and you never need to swap them between lenses. In any case, there are few filters you are likely to want to use for the action shots. And you can always have a holder in reserve for when you need special filters, especially for static shots.

Some special lenses, including the larger and faster telephotos and some fisheyes, use special slot-in filters which actually go behind most of the lens elements. If you've seen the size of the front element of a 300 mm $f2.8$ lens, you'll know why they do this — there is just no way you are going to get a filter that big. Putting them at the rear of the lens means they can be small — 39 mm is a typical size. With some fisheyes, however, the filters are a custom size and fit, and you can use only the ones supplied with the lens — typically amber, light blue, orange and UV. Rear-mounted filters are usually included in the optical design of the lens, so you must have one in place at all times, even if it is just a plain glass or UV filter.

A useful kit would consist of the following:

- 81A amber filters for warming — preferably a few of these so that you can have one on every lens on dull days.
- 82A light blue filters for slight correction in tungsten lighting.
- 80A deep blue filters for proper correction in tungsten lighting.
- Fluorescent-Day magenta filter to get rid of the green cast caused by strip lights.
- Polarising.
- Graduated — in a variety of colours, with blue and grey being the most useful.
- UV filters on all lenses for protection.

THE KIT

We've looked at the main components of the required kit individually. Now let's think about putting them together to create a basic aviation photographer's outfit.

LENSES

There is no one 'ideal' combination of lenses — it's very much a matter of personal taste. That said, a 28 mm or 35 mm wide angle, 70–210 mm zoom and 300 mm telephoto will provide you will a very solid base. You can add longer, faster and wider lenses to suit. And if you don't like zooms — perhaps because you want faster lenses — then you could replace the 70–210 mm with fixed 85 mm and 200 mm lenses.

EXTRA BODIES

Having talked you into buying a nice, expensive SLR, here is the bad news — you need two of them, or maybe even three! Once you have more lenses than cameras you can guarantee that the lens you want is the one in the camera bag. Having more than one camera body allows you to swap lenses very quickly — as fast as it takes to put down one camera and pick up another. It also reduces the risk of running out of film at the crucial moment, in that you can quickly switch to another body. Finally, if you don't find you have any of those problems, you can have different film stocks in the cameras — colour in one, mono in the other, for instance — or fast film in one for hangar or action shots and a medium speed emulsion in the other for general outdoor shots. Incidentally, it is worth having identical cameras. Continually switching from one camera to another can leave you groping for a crucially-needed control, with the risk of missing the shot, if the cameras don't match.

CAMERA BAGS & JACKETS

What you use to carry your gear is completely a matter of personal choice. At least one, highly-respected professional photographer has been known to carry a body and a couple of lenses in a plastic shopping bag. But then she wasn't trying to photograph aeroplanes.

Bear in mind that you need to work fast. If you use a bag, choose one with easy access to the equipment. It helps if you can get to the stuff without having to put the bag down — hard cases, especially those briefcase-type metal ones, score very badly in this respect. The only advantage of a metal case, in this kind of work, is as something to stand on if you need to peer over someone's shoulder. Otherwise, soft bags tend to be more useful.

Even better, if you don't mind looking a little strange, are those photographer's vests — like sleeveless safari jackets — which distribute the weight evenly and provide rapid access to all the gear. Make sure you get one that has pockets large enough for all but your longest telephotos.

METERS

The exposure meters built into cameras are so sophisticated these days that it seems perverse in the extreme to consider buying a separate, hand-held meter. And it's true that it offers few benefits for most photographers. Yet, as we will see when we discuss exposure techniques, a hand-held meter can get you out of trouble. All the same, for most people — and especially for those whose main interest is in photographing aeroplanes — it is worth considering only when you can't think of anything else to spend your money on.

A spot meter, which is capable of reading just a tiny part of the subject, and comes with its own viewfinder, is a powerful tool in the hands of the knowledgeable. It avoids problems with small highlights fooling the meter (you just aim it at another spot) and with getting the right exposure for a small object. Mind you, to get any real benefit from such a device, you have to know a lot about exposure and film, and for most photographers, amateur and professional, it's an unjustifiable expense.

PHOTOGRAPHIC BITS

Most modern electronic marvels become instantly less than marvellous when the batteries die. Cameras with electronic shutters, autofocus and metering systems are a case in point. Some might still give you a single mechanical shutter speed when the power goes, but you won't have the benefit of an exposure meter. If you have a highly automated and sophisticated camera, you're likely to be left with a totally dead machine: no longer a technological miracle, it now has all the utility of a doorstop.

If you carry more than one camera, you would have to be very unlucky indeed to have all the batteries fail at the same time, so the multi-body user does have some insurance. But it happens, and it can be highly embarrassing in the middle of a session which has taken a lot of time and effort — and perhaps even money — to set up.

The point of this preamble is to say that you should always carry spare batteries. And if they've been sitting in your camera bag for nine months or so, replace them. Batteries go off even when they're not being used, and there's little point changing one set of dead cells for another exactly the same. Some photographers like to carry one body which is totally mechanical, which is why Nikon's FM-2 has lasted so long. But you might find this a rather expensive solution.

Dust is one of your biggest enemies. When it coats the lens it results in softer, diffused images. When it gets onto the camera it's not long before it works its way inside, with the potential to cause mechanical failures and scratches on the film. And the aviation photographer spends a lot of time working in dusty environments.

The frequent use of a soft brush to get rid of the dust can avoid problems later. You can pay a lot for photographic brushes, but you are better off with a large make-up brush — the type used for applying powder and blusher. These are soft and huge, which is ideal for lenses. Some of the nooks and crannies might still resist its charms, and something stiffer might be required. An artist's paintbrush — the stiff-bristled type intended for oil painting — with the handle cut down is best for this work.

As a supplement to the brush you can use canned air to get rid of the offending particles. Be careful to keep the can out of direct sunlight, and always make the first squirt, after taking it out of your camera bag, away from your camera into the air. Once shaken-up, the spray might give out a brief liquid jet rather than gas.

The final bit of photographic gear is something without which many a budding photographic career would have perished — gaffer tape. This is a fabric-based self-adhesive tape which is used for everything from sticking gelatin filters over lenses to providing the last bit of security for a camera stuck out on the wing. It is robust stuff, capable of sticking to almost anything, yet coming off easily when you need it to. There should always be a roll of gaffer tape — or duct tape, which is similar — in your kit-bag. It now comes in a variety of colours, but it's best to go for black as this avoids potential problems with reflections in canopies, paintwork and so on.

EXTRA GOODIES

Success in taking pictures of moving aeroplanes is often a matter of being prepared and anticipating when the best shots are likely to happen. So one of the most invaluable tools is not a piece of photographic equipment at all, but a radio.

Portable radios capable of picking up air traffic, or airband, frequencies are pretty common these days. Cheap versions are available for not much more than the cost of a roll of film. All they are is a standard radio tuned to different VHF frequencies.

With the radio tuned to the local tower frequency at an air show, you will hear when aircraft are coming in, and get some idea of what they are about to do.

More sophisticated versions are capable of scanning. Rather than you having to tune the radio manually, the set monitors the various frequencies and can pick out those in use. This is very handy when you don't know which frequencies are being employed, or if you want to switch between several frequencies. Pre-programming is also available, which means you can have a known frequency available at the touch of a button while scanning the other channels. Naturally, all this costs more. A good scanner, such as those made by Sony, will set you back the price of a reasonable SLR camera. Whether it is worth the expense is up to you. Next time you go to an air show, try positioning yourself next to someone who is using a scanner, and see how much benefit you derive from it.

If you are not a pilot, it is a good idea to learn some of the jargon, if you want to get the most out of what you're hearing. Regulatory bodies, such as the CAA (in the UK) and the FAA (in the US) publish their own guides to radiotelephony, and independent publishers are a good source of tutorial manuals.

Two-way radios, or transceivers, have their uses too. In air-to-air photography, it's quite useful for the photographer to be in direct contact with the pilot of the other aircraft. And the same is true for ground-to-air work, where the pilot is putting on a display just for you.

At air shows, however, transceivers are not necessary, and can be potentially dangerous. There is little reason for you to speak to either pilots or tower at a show, and accidentally keying the microphone (which does happen) can blot out radio traffic for those people who really need it. You shouldn't even consider using a transceiver at an airport.

In many countries, you need a valid radiotelephony licence in order to use an airband transceiver, and shops may demand to see one before selling you the equipment. The licence is usually an extra rating added to a pilot's licence, following the completion of a short course and the (successful) taking of a simple exam. Even if you are not a pilot, it may be worth finding out if you can obtain the licence, if you intend doing a lot of air-to-air work. Your local flying school should be able to help you out. In some countries a licence is required even for an airband receiver. However, in the UK and USA you should not run into legal problems unless you start using the information you gather for nefarious purposes.

Military traffic is usually on UHF bands, unless it is in contact with other VHF users, so you're still not likely to pick it up.

Be careful where you take these radios. In some countries, even apparently quite civilised ones, just the ownership of a camera and a spotter's guide is enough to have you branded as a spy. A special radio would be conclusive proof of your espionage activities, and your stay might turn out to be somewhat longer than you had anticipated!

As well as hearing what is about to happen, it's also useful to see what's coming. A pair of binoculars will help you identify distant aircraft and generally help you stay informed about what is happening around you.

For this kind of work you want to avoid binoculars with huge front elements. You simply don't need their light-gathering abilities, and you certainly don't want their bulk and weight —you've got enough to lug around with your photographic gear. Similarly, high-magnification optics are unnecessary, and even self-defeating. Although theoretically capable of resolving every whisker of the pilot's moustache, the simultaneous magnification of hand tremors and general vibration means that you will actually see less than someone using less powerful optics.

The answer is a pair of compact binoculars — 8 x 25 is ideal. People such as Minolta, Nikon and Leitz make some superb compact designs which can easily slip into a shirt or jacket pocket.

NOTEBOOK
A small notebook has several uses. If you are the fastidious type, you can keep a record of any special techniques or exposures you

might have used. At the very least, it's worth noting down the general exposure levels you are using, and your most common shutter speeds and apertures on the day. That way you can sort out any problems that might crop up in the pictures later — if the shots are blurred, for example, it could be enlightening to realise you were using a shutter speed of 1/30th.

An even better use for the notebook is to keep track of the aircraft. If there are any types you don't know, the time to find out is when you take the shot. Ask the crew, if you can. Ask the person next to you (the one with all the badges who loudly intones the serial number and engine type of every passing aircraft). And listen out for information from the announcers. This is by far the easiest time to get the information you need, which could prove essential if you try to sell your pictures.

Instead of a notebook you could use a small tape recorder — a pocket-sized dictating machine or a personal hif-fi which is capable of recording: but only if speaking into a machine in public doesn't make you feel a complete idiot. The biggest drawback with tape recorders, apart from the damage to your public image, is that you have to be very disciplined about transcribing the tapes. And it has to be done soon after the event so that you can remember what is meant by the more cryptic grunts, squeaks and groans that inevitably populate the tape.

If your aircraft recognition skills are a bit rusty, some kind of spotter's book can come in handy for identifying the more obscure types. However, the usual perverse laws of the universe dictate that the puzzling aircraft in front of you is the only one the author missed out of the book.

EAR DEFENDERS

At air shows, you are normally sufficiently far back from the aircraft for noise to be, if not exactly comfortable, at least not a health hazard. This does not necessarily apply elsewhere, however.

If you are a guest at a military establishment, you will normally be provided with ear protection whenever you go on to the flightline, or other areas where noise can reach painful or damaging levels. Use it! Even when the sound level seems bearable, it can be doing you a lot of damage.

Elsewhere, looking after your ears is completely your own responsibility. So it is worth investing in a set of ear defenders. If you need protection very rarely, or don't think you will ever be in that kind of situation, it's still worth having some ordinary earplugs, of the kind you can get from the chemist. And even if you have got some proper ear defenders, put a pack of plugs in your camera bag as well — you never know when you're going to forget the defenders.

MISCELLANEOUS

A press card can be a useful item, getting you into restricted areas, but it's a waste of time buying the things you see advertised in the backs of photography magazines. Anyone likely to want to see a press card will know what a real one looks like. To get a real one you normally have to belong to a newspaper, publishing house or professional body. And most major events require additional identification, in the form of letters of accreditation from publishers or magazines.

The idea of carrying furniture around with you might seem odd, but a collapsible stool, like those used for fishing, will give you something to sit on when you are at an air show and, if it's stable, something to stand on to see static exhibits or passing aircraft over people's heads. A slightly higher viewpoint can give you a better angle for static aircraft, so if your car is going to be parked fairly near, you might like to think about bringing along a set of kitchen steps. You won't want to carry them around all day, but you can easily fetch them for the static shots. The same car could also contain a collapsible garden chair for watching the show and a cool box packed with drinks for surviving it. If you just need something to rest on when life gets too hard, a shooting stick is more compact.

The last piece of non-photographic kit is for those lucky enough to go up in some kind of high-performance aeroplane. When you're being thrown around the sky it's very easy to start feeling somewhat queasy. First-time travellers in jet fighters nearly always get a second look at their breakfasts. The situation is made worse by looking through the viewfinder. Being able to see just a small portion of the world robs you of many of the visual clues which would normally help your brain overcome motion sickness.

Having a *full* breakfast helps, which comes as a surprise to many people. The worst thing you can do is have just a little to eat — it sloshes around in your stomach making matters ten times worse. A full stomach is much less prone to sickness, providing, of course, that the food itself didn't make you feel ill. But it's always worth helping nature a bit with some motion sickness tablets, taken before you start your ride. And you could take a sick bag in case that is still not enough.

EQUIPMENT CARE

Having bought all this expensive equipment, it pays to keep it in good condition. This is easier said than done when you are standing on a windy airfield, bathed in prop-wash, being relentlessly blasted by dust, grit, oil and exhaust fumes while trying to change lenses, load film and fit filters. Oh well, no one said it was going to be easy.

Looking after your equipment is largely a matter of common sense — keeping it out of the rain, away from sources of heat and out of the path of taxying aircraft, that kind of thing. However, the aviation photographer is faced with some special hazards which are worth considering.

The main one is all that dust flying around. With the artificial breezes created by prop- and jet-wash, and the fact that airfields tend to be the worst places in the world for flying debris, you have to pay special attention to keeping your camera grit free.

If dirt gets into the film compartment it can clog up the camera and leave potentially disastrous scratch marks on your pictures, as the film gets pulled over the pieces of grit. So don't open the camera back in the middle of a dust cloud. Keep it open for the minimum amount of time while changing film, although it is worth taking a second to give the back a quick once-over with compressed air (but *not* on the shutter itself) or a soft brush.

Similar rules apply when changing lenses. Don't use compressed air on the reflex mirror as this can damage the coatings. Use of a very soft brush is fine, but if the marks persist it may mean a trip to your local repairers to get it cleaned.

In dry, dusty conditions, keep checking your lens. If the front element, or the UV filter if you have one, gets clogged it will degrade the image quality. A lens tissue or cloth is handy for removing the worst of the marks, but always give the lens a wipe with a soft brush first: this removes the worst pieces of grit and stops you grinding them into the glass and scratching it. In any case, never rub hard on any lens or filter surfaces. It's worth having a few spare UV filters in case your current ones get so clogged up that you can't easily clean them.

PROFILE: GEORGE HALL

For most of us, getting to photograph fast jets is a treat. For George Hall it is both a job and a way of life. This San Francisco-based photographer makes a living out of shooting aeroplanes, and specializes in stunning pictures of military jets.

George first picked up a camera while recovering from injuries sustained in Vietnam. Like many top professionals he is largely self-taught. But he did have some training which still proves invaluable: having been in the Army, he understands the military mind — something he has to deal with every day.

He became a professional photographer in 1970, originally taking pictures of the ground for land and real estate companies, from aircraft and helicopters, something he still does from time to time. For most of the 1970s he was the US photographer for the Goodyear blimp. The turning point came towards the end of the decade when a new US publisher, Presidio Press, asked him to take pictures of carrier aviation. They liked the results, and other books on the US Air Force in Europe and Red Flag followed. This was in the early '80s, and George discovered there was a strong stock photography market for these images. As a result he decided to concentrate almost exclusively on military aviation.

George has a private pilot's licence and enjoys getting in a little 'stick time' when he takes a ride in a military jet. Although not essential, he feels it helps: 'It certainly helps to know the subject — you couldn't be a soccer photographer without knowing the game: you wouldn't know what was going to happen. You have to know what airplanes are capable of and you have to know your terminology and be able to converse intelligently with people. And I can't help thinking that it's good for them to realize that you know something about your subject. Some guy who's got you in the back seat of his jet would like to know you've done it before, and you're not going to freak out and cause him any kind of difficulty . . .'

GETTING PERMISSION

Before he gets to that point, however, George has to go through the ritual of setting up the photo session. Dealing with the military bureaucracy has been a tough skill to master.

'It's funny. You'd think it would get better — but it doesn't. Setting things up is easily 90–95 per cent of what I do — writing people letters, talking on the phone, getting permission to do things, which is very difficult with the military, even though they know me: calling the same people over and over and over again, double and triple checking that what they've said is arranged is indeed arranged. I've arrived on the scene too many times and it's like you're from Mars. You get there and supposedly everything's set up and nobody's heard of you.

This is the kind of shot which has to be carefully set up. The airfield was closed so that George could shoot pictures for USAir. He positioned himself at the end of the runway with a 300 mm lens. The Boeing 737 had just cleared the deck and the wheels were coming up. The pilot then held the aircraft low, making it a memorable occasion for all concerned!

'The US military get a lot of people who are hobbyists, tailspotters, who want to get on bases, they want to get on the tarmac, they want to get out by the runway, they want to get up in a tanker, they want to get up in a jet — I mean, of course they do — but that doesn't mean they're going to. The big American bases are deluged with requests. Generally speaking there's not really any way to do it unless you have a pretty good hook with a magazine or a book project. And it's got to be real . . .

'Actually, it's always a sort of love-hate relationship between the military and the press. On the one hand, they're very conscious of telling their story and getting the word out on particular programs that they're interested in promoting. On the other hand, there is always the possibility you might be out to do a hatchet job. But if you're coming in doing a book on carriers in the '90s and they're trying to get two more carrier battle groups, at a cost of $3 billion each against a resistant Congress, they're going to be real interested in a nice book. If you're trying to do a book on something that's not current, not of interest to them, or something they're letting die, they might not be as co-operative.

'I subscribe to ten or fifteen different periodicals, everything from the *Wall Street Journal* to all the military and defence publications, and read to see who's got what contracts. If I hear someone has just signed on to the F-14 as a new contractor I'll make sure I get hold of those people and say: "By the way, I've got a lot of great F-14 slides".'

EQUIPMENT

In just the 35 mm format alone, George uses as many as ten bodies and twenty lenses, ranging from fisheye to 600 mm, to help him get the shot. But the actual gear he carries with him varies according to the job in hand.

'I operate on several different levels depending what the shoot is. If I go up in a jet, for instance, I take very little more than the rankest amateur tourist has with him. There's not very much room — you can't take a big bag of stuff in any of the jets except perhaps the F-15. I always take two cameras because you don't want to get up there on the flight of a lifetime only to have your camera break. I seldom take more than three lenses — no bag, I just take the cameras and lenses and keep them between my legs or whatever. I have an Air Force flight suit that has pockets all over — I stuff all the film and lenses in the pockets.

'If I'm doing something larger, where we're going to go flying in a tanker, we're going to go flying in a jet, we're going to shoot airplanes coming overhead from the ground, shoot airplanes on static that are parked around the field, and we're also going to do other things — we're going to shoot inside the control tower, inside the air traffic control room, perhaps a classroom at Top Gun where we'll need some strobes for portraits of pilots — this is not just an aviation job now, it's more of an industrial, corporate type shoot.

'To do something like this, I'll go to the other extreme. I have a whole vehicle, a little Ford van, that is set up as a travelling shooting vehicle. It's fully equipped with cameras in several formats, 12,000 watts worth of strobes, and a generator for AC. It has a custom-built rack on the roof that two people can stand on. We carry a full complement of diffusion screens, stands and fabrics, 1,000 feet of extension cord, a step ladder, and walkie talkies. We can light any situation. I could light a B-1 at night.'

Although he has the Pentax 6 x 7 cm kit, George is pretty much a devotee of 35 mm. 'You get real spoiled using 35s because they are fast and portable. You can shoot a lot of film in a short time. When you're shooting a stunt aircraft that's doing lomcovaks or something, there's no substitute for having four or five frames a second on your Nikon. I'd be lucky to get two shots in that period of time with the 6 x 7. It's hard to make yourself go to such a deliberate camera, unless you're doing a deliberate shot, like a static shot of a jet parked at sunset, that kind of thing. That's where it's nice to put your 6 x 7 on a tripod, and maybe do a Polaroid test.

A classic ground-to-air shot. George used a 400 mm lens for this picture of a Canadian CF-18. The Hornet was dogfighting with F-14s, and George carefully chose the moment when the aircraft pulled 7 *g*s, creating streams of condensation

'I'd much rather use 35 mm in a jet where I can shoot a lot of film. I sometimes only have 12–13 minutes in the whole flight to shoot. With the 35 mm I can shoot much more. It's important for stock and for getting that decisive shot. If the guy's rolling the airplane around, you've got to be a better shooter than I am to hit that decisive moment with your 6 x 7 where he's just in the right position. I'm the first to admit that I rely on high-speed, six frames a second motors to shoot a lot of film.

'I have a whole range of lenses for the 6 x 7, including a 400 mm *f*4, which is sort of like having a 200 mm on your Nikon when it's on the Pentax, but you can use that same lens with a special mount on a 35 mm camera and it becomes a very nice long lens that costs about a third of a Nikon 400 mm *f*3.5.'

For air-to-air work, where he's riding in the back seat of a jet, George's choice of lenses is very simple: 'I use the 50 mm a lot in the jets. And I use wider lenses. A wide angle is nice because you can get a piece of your airplane, your wing or tail in the picture. I'll often take a very wide lens, like a 16 mm fisheye or a 20 mm, which I use with a remote cable release — an electric cable release — so I can shoot myself. I can prop it up on the dash or hold it at arm's length and get a shot of me with my mask on and my visor down — you can't tell it's me and it becomes a useful generic shot of a fighter pilot. Nobody knows it's the guy in the back seat. To most people it looks like the real thing. I'll do that on almost every flight, and I'll be careful to do that while we're on the right heading so the light is in my face. And I'll have the pilot do something with the airplane — some steep aileron rolls so that the horizon isn't just boring and flat.

'I never use anything much longer than 85 mm. I found out the hard way that when using lenses like 200 mm, your stuff is never sharp, because you're getting a lot of unavoidable diffusion in the canopy.'

From the ground it's a different story: 'If I'm going to be out shooting at an air show, I take a lot of long lenses. And by long I mean 300, 400, 500, 600 mm lenses. I very seldom use the 600 mm because it's too hard to hand-hold and it's also too hard to use on a tripod. But I do use the 400 and 500 mm lenses fairly routinely to shoot air show demonstrations from the ground — seldom under 200 mm as the guy's never that close.

'That's a major hunk of stuff to carry, so I have a little wheeled cart — it's sort of an industrial-strength version of an airport baggage cart with big wheels, and I put all my stuff on to that cart with bungees and drag it all out on to the runway.'

You will seldom see George's lenses sporting filters. 'I've never liked the idea of putting anything in front of the lens if I can avoid it. I already shoot through glass canopies half the time.'

SPECIAL KIT

People often suspect that professionals use some kind of special cameras, unavailable and even unknown to the general public. This is sometimes true in other branches of photography where customised gear is necessary. But aviation photographers use the same kind of cameras as everyone else, although the means of carrying and firing them may be a little different at times.

'It's remarkable that most of what I do is not with special stuff. The cameras that I take in the jets are not modified in any way. It's off-the-shelf Nikon gear.

'The major exception is a camera pod which mounts on the underwing hard point of a military jet. Most military jets have universal hard points under their wings and on the centre line where they can hang weapons, gas tanks, electronics or baggage pods. It's a 14-inch spacing between the lugs — the Russians have the same thing. Second World War aircraft had the same thing. This pod will go on any airplane with 14-inch hardware, which is practically any tactical airplane in the NATO military. It can hold up to four or five different cameras looking straight out the back, straight out the front, straight down, or inward or outward. I've run 120-format cameras and I've put video cameras in the pod too. The pod was used on the *Top Gun* movie with a film camera. But mostly I just shoot stills with 35 mm.

'The cameras are radio controlled, so there's no wiring. It has its own power and there's no hook-up. It just goes right on the hard point. It takes five seconds to put it on the airplane. If I'm in the back seat I'll have the radio to fire the cameras off. Or, in many cases, I'll send it up on a single-seat airplane and brief the pilot what to do. They'll go and get their shots and I'll just take the film out — and hope they did what I told them. Or with the radio, I can be in the airplane that's being shot — I've done a lot of shots where the guy in the back seat in the picture is me. Or I can be in a third airplane, for that matter, or I can be on the ground. I've shot the Blue Angels at an air show where they were directly overhead. They're much too busy to be taking pictures during their show. I just stood on the ground with the radio — it has a long range — and I took the pictures while watching the show; kind of like flying a radio-controlled model airplane!

For this shot of an F-15 Eagle, George shot through the canopy of his own aircraft using a 50 mm lens. The late evening light turns an otherwise ordinary air-to-air shot into something spectacular

'It's commercial FM two-way radio, much like the police would have. It's a very sophisticated radio, impervious to extra kinds of RF. It can't be overwhelmed by a lot of radar energy, something like that. It won't make the cameras go off falsely which a cheaper radio like a little model airplane radio would do, some of which are quite sophisticated, but would tend to be overwhelmed — a lot of radio or RF energy would cause them to chatter. There's a little tone decoder that has a tone for each camera and a telephone touch-tone pad with a button for each camera. Each time I push button five, that camera goes off.'

TECHNIQUE

Although his kit includes zoom lenses, and he is starting to use a 35–105 mm to cut down the number of lenses he carries during flights, George mainly sticks to fixed focal length optics. 'What I do is, instead of using a zoom lens, I just zoom the other airplane in. You've got to learn to tell the guy to get where you want. He'll usually do it. Pilots love getting their pictures taken. And in the military they're used to very precise formation flying. Tell them where you want them and that's where they'll be.

'I don't think I've ever gone on a photo mission that has been nothing but a photo mission. They just don't do that. It's too expensive to fly these airplanes. They're going to ask you to go along on a scheduled training flight. You have to squeeze your shots into the trip out to the range and back, or to the carrier and back, and then for the bulk of the flight, for thirty or forty minutes, you're just going to have to sit still in the back seat while the people do whatever it is they're up for, whether its intercepts or fighter manoeuvres or dropping bombs or refuelling or whatever it is.

'Now, in some cases, like with refuelling, you can get some real interesting stuff while they're doing that. In some other stuff like intercepts, where you're up all alone in the sky and you're intercepting some other guy twenty miles away on radar, you're probably just going to sit back and play with the radar until they're done and you hook up for your formation to fly back. And for that 10–15 minutes going back to the base, that's when you get your pictures. So frequently, on an hour, hour-and-a-half flight, I'm only shooting ten minutes, twelve minutes, something like that.'

A self portrait with a 16 mm fisheye lens, in the back seat of an F-16.

Most of the work is done in setting up and planning the session. Once airborne, the photography itself is pretty straightforward.

'Generally speaking, if you get up with the airplanes you want, and it's a nice day, and you can manage to get up at one end of the day or the other, and you get some nice clouds — there's a lot of things that you don't have any control over, like pretty skies and so forth — and you have the right cameras with you and everything's working, you'll get pretty good shots.'

The biggest problem used to be the ride itself: 'The environment in the jet is real unpleasant, and it takes some getting used to. Just about anybody, the first time he goes in a jet, is not going to get many pictures. He'll experience high *g*s, unusual attitudes and claustrophobia, and he's going to spend the whole time being very uncomfortable until he gets used to it.

'I've had people say to me, in sort of a sour grapes way: "If I were up in the back seat then I would have got the same shot." And my answer is: "You're right, you would have, but you weren't up in the back seat and I was, and that's the hard part." '

George Hall's most unusual piece of equipment is the pod. This attaches to standard NATO hardpoints on aircraft and radio-controlled firing of its cameras makes possible shots like this

TECHNIQUE

It's pointless having all the equipment if you can't use it properly. Advertising for the latest generation of cameras would have you believe that all you have to do is take the camera along to any event and the sophisticated electronics will handle matters from there.

Happily, things haven't got that bad yet. Even with all their advanced electronics, cameras are incapable of choosing their subjects and arranging them into attractive pictures (although the camera companies are working on it). Even the technical stuff, such as deciding on the best exposure and focusing the lens, is far from perfect. Automatic systems which do this kind of thing are good, but not infallible, and aviation photography poses especially difficult problems for them. So it's just as well to know what's going on, and be able to correct it when necessary. But before we get on to technicalities, let's have a look at the bit which is entirely up to you — composition.

COMPOSITION AND VIEWPOINT

It is virtually impossible to teach good composition, especially from a book. There are all kinds of perceived wisdom, from the 'thirds' rule (where the main horizontal and vertical elements of the picture should fall a third of the way across the frame) to the hoary old myth of 'always have something red in the picture'.

Sticking to any kind of hard-and-fast rule leads to boring and predictable pictures. Each shot has to be assessed individually, and you shouldn't be afraid to experiment, and be outrageous. That said, it's time to lay down a few rules! Actually, they are nothing more than tips, culled from long experience, and are intended merely to help you avoid common mistakes while you are developing your own style. Perhaps the best piece of advice is to realize that good shots don't necessarily fall into your lap — you have to be prepared to work for them.

The first practical tip is to watch what you are doing with the edges of the frame. While you are busy concentrating on the main part of the subject at or near the centre of the picture, you can be doing nasty things further out. Just like people, aeroplanes just don't look right when their heads and feet are cut off. Clipping off just the tips of wings, tails, noses and undercarriage looks messy and uncomfortable. It's much better to either get the whole thing in, or make the amputation more deliberate. For example, when you are shooting from slightly to one side, rather than get just half or three-quarters of both wings in, it may be better to get all of the more distant wing and crop the nearest one near the root.

The other point to consider about the frame is what to have in it. Take a quick look around the image and decide whether you

Below: Getting close with a wide angle creates distortion (top), which is avoided by stepping back and using a medium wide angle or standard lens (bottom)

want all those things in your shot. What does each object add to the picture? If the answer is 'nothing', is there any way of getting rid of it? The corollary of this approach is that it is often best to fill the frame with your main subject.

You may complain that this is easier said than done, and that's true. The aviation photographer's life seems to be filled with attempts to make the subject larger in the frame — that's why we invite hernias by lugging around huge lenses. If, for any reason, the aircraft absolutely *must* be small in the frame — and this applies mainly to airborne craft — then look for something else to introduce into the picture which complements the aeroplane: another aeroplane, a hangar or some other ground detail, and perhaps the ground itself.

Make use of any vantage points; the airfield control tower is often a good place to shoot from if it has an outside walkway to avoid photographing through glass. Tall buildings or the tops of hangars are useful too, but make sure you are safe and have permission.

A high viewpoint like this presents the aircraft against a

Low angles can obscure canopies, but if the aircraft is reasonably recognizable and the composition is otherwise attractive, this might not matter

background of tarmac, grass or runway, which makes a pleasant change from skies and skylines. But it does tend to put a fair distance between you and the aircraft.

Mind you, your problems don't always end when you do manage to get close. Aircraft may look beautiful in the sky, but on the ground, and through the viewfinder of a camera, they become strange angular things, wilfully incompatible with any picture format you care to think of.

Static aircraft can cause some real headaches simply from where they are sitting. Occasionally, you may come across an aircraft which is sitting in splendid isolation, free of picture pollutants such as people, ladders, fuel bowsers and so on. But look again, beyond the aeroplane itself. More often than not there are pylons, buildings, people or other nasty objects apparently sprouting from the cockpit. Even worse, there may be bits of other aircraft, which are a particular headache because they are likely to be the same general colour and shade as your subject: in the picture these protrusions may, at best, confuse the outline of your aeroplane, and might even look as if they are part of it.

So watch the background, and before you press the button, run your eye around the outline of your subject to check for foreign matter. If there is objectionable background detail, try moving to your left or right. If that doesn't work, a lower or higher viewpoint can get rid of it. You could also switch to a wider lens and move in closer; this alters the relative sizes of near and distant objects, with those that are closer growing in the frame while distant objects shrink into insignificance or disappear altogether behind your main subject.

It is amazing how easily foreign objects can creep into your shots. You may think you've tightened up the composition so that there are no unwanted objects in it. But a slight shift in viewpoint can introduce new and previously unnoticed nasties. So keep your eyes open *before* you raise the camera. Know what ·is around you, and what might find its way into the shot.

There is one other reason for keeping an eye on the background, and that's to keep your pictures on the straight and level. Shooting aircraft on the ground, especially tail-draggers which sit at an angle, can easily lead to sloping horizons. You are so busy lining up the subject that you forget about the background, and even when everything appears fine in the viewfinder, the result can look very uncomfortable in the final picture. If you are making prints from negatives there is some scope for correction, although it does involve slicing off the outer edges of the shot. With transparencies you may have real problems, So have a quick glance at the horizon before shooting: a 'grid'-type focusing screen can help.

The foreground needs to be watched, too. Vast expanses of empty ground can be dull and even ugly. The best solution is often to fill it with something: the aircraft's shadow comes in handy sometimes, as do ground support equipment, runway or ramp markings or reflections in wet ground. Using a low viewpoint might get rid of it but can introduce other problems. The wings can easily blot out important details of the aircraft, including the canopy and markings. The opposite approach — using a high viewpoint — not only allows you to fill the frame more easily with the aircraft, but also shows up these details.

The same principle applies in other situations, too. Even when the subject is airborne, it's not always possible to fill the frame comfortably just with the aircraft by itself, so look for something else — another aircraft, hills in the background, smoke or vapour trails — to occupy the blank space.

On the other hand, you might have something in the frame you *don't* want, such as other people, bits of equipment or — in the case of air-to-air shots — bits of your own aircraft. The rule is: If you can't get rid of it, use it! Or at least put it somewhere it won't be noticed.

DISTORTION

A common problem with any lens other than the 'standard' is one of subject distortion. Even leaving aside lens aberrations, such as barrel and pincushion distortion, the normal effects of different focal lengths can be difficult to handle.

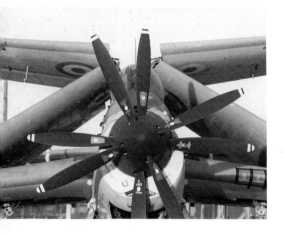

Getting back further still and shooting from a distance with a long lens squashes the subject. This can be used to good effect with strong patterns

It's sometimes said that wide angle lenses exaggerate perspective, while telephotos compress it. That's not strictly true. There is only one thing which has any effect on perspective, and that is where you stand. Your viewpoint determines the distance from you to the various parts of the subject. However, a wide angle does include more of the scene, particularly foreground details, and it does invite you to stand closer. Telephotos, on the other hand, are generally used to extract small portions of distant scenes.

Shooting from a wingtip with a 24 mm lens will highly exaggerate the size and shape of the wing. Indeed, the same goes for shooting from any angle — one part or another is going to be distorted. There is nothing intrinsically wrong with that, and if handled skilfully it can produce a very attractive and dramatic picture. But there are dangers.

Below (left): Watch for cropping the edges of the aircraft, particularly on grabbed shots. Slight cropping is worse than cutting out, say, the entire tail. (Right): If the frame is filled, slight cropping of wheels and other extremities isn't so noticeable

The shape of an aircraft is a vital component of its charm and attraction to enthusiasts. Bend the wing of a Spitfire out of shape and viewers may feel uncomfortable, unhappy or, worst of all, baffled. In other words, you could make the aircraft totally unrecognisable.

How much that matters depends entirely on the purpose of your photography. If you are shooting for your personal pleasure, and you are simply after good pictures, then there is no problem. However, if your main interest is in the aircraft, and particularly if you want to share the pictures with other aviation enthusiasts, then changing the personality of an aircraft through lens distortion is probably unacceptable.

One way of lessening the distortion of wide angles, while helping to fill the frame more effectively, is to get high. Short of taking along your own cherry picker, or tree, this means using anything to hand — climbing on to a truck or trailer, for example. Even standing in the open doorway of a car can help.

By and large, aircraft look most natural when shot with standard to telephoto length lenses, and for one very good reason. To use these lenses you will have to put some distance between you and the machinery — a distance which is not dissimilar to the sort of range from which we are used to viewing aircraft. Distortion problems are generally avoided, the aircraft looks 'normal' and it's often easier to compose the shot without the large, awkward areas of ground and sky that wide angles seem to suck in.

This is not to say that telephotos are free from distortion. Distant objects always look closer together than they really are — a sort of squashing effect known as 'flat perspective'. Telephotos exaggerate this by narrowing down the view to just those distant scenes. This again can distort the shape of an aircraft, making it appear flat and strangely angular. More often, however, the effect simply adds a bit of drama and can be very effective with large aircraft if they have a smaller aeroplane or other object in front of them.

Ironically, most of the objections to wide angles disappear when you get really close. For shooting cockpit interiors, a wide angle of some description is essential — 24 mm is a good place to start, but you might need something even wider for more cramped cockpits. And something like a 35 mm or 24 mm is useful for shooting exterior details — engine close-ups, aircraft markings and so on. By working close with one of these lenses you help to ensure that no one will walk in front of the camera at the crucial moment. And if some background detail does creep into the shot, it tends to be small and insignificant.

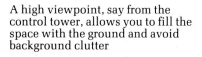

A high viewpoint, say from the control tower, allows you to fill the space with the ground and avoid background clutter

CROPPING

Photographers who print their own pictures have one advantage over transparency users in that they can easily crop their pictures to suit the subject. Wide, shallow pictures can be highly effective, if you are careful not to overdo it. Cropping pictures in that way is fine for your own consumption, but is not really advisable if you are trying to sell your pictures. Magazine and book editors tend to prefer standard-format pictures, which they can crop themselves, if necessary.

There is also a tendency to use cropping to save an otherwise dull or unsuccessful picture. If you find yourself resorting to this kind of tactic it is usually best to give up on the picture and resolve to try harder next time.

FOCUSING

One of the major worries of anyone shooting action pictures is getting the subject sharp. To get the full impact from your pictures they need to be perfectly crisp — sharp pictures look better and sell better.

Alas, focusing on a lump of metal, moving at 500 mph is a significantly more demanding and difficult than getting your cat crisp in the frame. By the time you have fiddled around with the focusing, erring first towards one side of perfect focus and then the other, the aircraft has flown past, landed and been tied down for the night.

Static subjects are not such a problem, as far as getting the main point of focus right. But you will find that when you are close to an object, while the front might be sharp, the back is out of focus — or vice versa.

To help cover up any focusing inaccuracies with moving subjects, or to get the whole of a nearby subject sharp, photographers make use of a phenomenon known as depth of field.

A low viewpoint means that much of your background is often a plain, unobtrusive, sky

DEPTH OF FIELD

As focus is both critical and difficult, depth of field is an important ally of the aviation photographer. So it's worth considering the subject in a little more detail. Contrary to popular misconception, the terms 'depth of field' and 'depth of focus' are not interchangeable, although having a lot of each is undeniably useful. Depth of field relates to the subject, while depth of focus is to do with what happens inside the camera.

These phenomena are connected to the fact that no lens is perfect. An infinitely small dot of light coming from infinity will show up in the image not as a point but as a small disc of light, because of the limitations of optics. This disc is known as the 'circle of confusion' and places the ultimate limit on the resolution of the lens.

Now, for the sake of example, let's say you are using a 50 mm lens set to $f8$ and you have accurately focused on a subject at a distance of five metres. If it weren't for the deficiencies of optics, points on the main subject would show up in the image as points, while points on objects nearer to or further from the main subject would appear as progressively larger circles of confusion — making them out-of-focus. However, in real life this effect starts showing up only after these circles have exceeded the limiting circle of confusion. In other words, nearer and farther objects will appear as sharp as the main subject — up to a point. This is depth of field.

As a side note, it's worth mentioning that the size of the limiting circle of confusion is a fairly arbitrary figure. A point of light is said to be in focus if its circle of confusion is less than a certain size: this used to be — and often still is — set at either 0.05 mm or the focal length of the lens divided by 1,000. A more realistic figure, in these days of high resolution films and lenses and small formats, is a fixed value of 0.033 mm.

The depth of field is calculated using the standard circle of confusion, the focal length of the lens, the distance to the focus

You can also fill empty space with other aircraft, sometimes providing two views of the same type in one shot

point and the lens aperture in use. In our example, the depth of field extends from 3.3 metres to 10.6 metres. You'll notice that this is 1.7 metres in front of the focus point and 5.6 metres behind it — the depth of field is always greater behind the object.

Opening the lens up one stop, to ƒ5.6, changes the depth of field. It now starts at 3.7 metres and goes out to 8.0 metres. Stopping down the lens to ƒ11 changes these figures to 2.9 metres and 18.3 metres. So you can see that the smaller the stop, the greater the depth of field.

When the lens was at ƒ8, focused at 5 metres, the total depth of field was 7.3 metres. If we focus on a closer point — say, 2 metres from the lens — the near and far points in focus are at 1.7 and 2.5 metres, a total depth of only 0.8 metres. Aiming at a point 10 metres away gives an image that is sharp all the way from 4.9 metres to infinity. So the further you are from the subject, the greater the depth of field.

That's probably enough figures: but similar things happen when you change the focal length. Shorter focal lengths have greater depth of field — indeed the depth on a 20 mm or wider ultra-wide lens can be so great that you hardly need to focus if you are using a reasonably small stop — ƒ8 or smaller.

The depth of field is usually marked on the lens. Either side of the mark showing the main focus point, you will find additional marks, either colour-coded or lined up with aperture numbers. These marks, when read off against the distance scale on the focus ring, indicate the depth of field at any given stop. They provide only a rough guide, and are sometimes a little optimistic, but they are enough to give you some idea of what's happening.

A better impression is gained by using a depth of field preview, if your camera has one. All viewing and metering through an SLR is done with the lens at its widest, brightest stop. The aperture closes down to its set value only when the shutter is about tõ open, and pops open again when the exposure has been made. On some cameras, however, it is possible to stop the lens down to its set value by pressing a button or lever. You can then see directly the depth of field you will get. It's still not perfect, as the image is dark and small, and it may be impossible to tell for sure whether an object is sharp, but it's a useful aid. This feature is rarely available on cameras using shutter-priority

Formation teams help to fill the frame, when one aircraft would be hopelessly small

or fully programmed exposure modes. This is because the aperture is not defined until the moment you make the exposure, as it depends on the light reading at the time. Manual and aperture priority modes create no such problems, however, as the lens is set to a definite stop.

In the rush and excitement of shooting moving aircraft, you are unlikely to have enough time to contemplate the intricacies of depth of field, which is why it's a good idea to play around with your lenses and get to know how much depth you can expect from them under different circumstances.

DEPTH OF FOCUS

Depth of focus is directly related to depth of field, but is concerned with the area of sharpness in front of and behind the film plane. In other words, it effectively defines how much you could move the film forwards or backwards before you see any loss of sharpness. The answer is — not much. Depth of focus tends to be quite small, but it does have some important practical ramifications. For one thing, a large depth of focus will cover up for any unevenness or inaccuracies in the lens mounting. But more important, it will avoid problems with film curvature. Film has a tendency to curl, which could — and occasionally does — result in the image going out of focus at the edges. Good quality cameras, including 35mm models, have pressure plates in the camera back to keep the film flat. Having plenty of depth of focus helps too, although the high quality of modern cameras means that it is more of academic than practical interest.

Depth of focus is also affected by changes in lens focal length, aperture and acceptable circle of confusion. In place of the focus distance, it is calculated using the distance between the lens and the film plane. When lenses are focused on closer objects they are moved away from the film. This actually *increases* depth of focus, which is the one area in which depth of focus differs from depth of field.

IN PRACTICE

What does all this mean for the aviation photographer? Well, action photography places conflicting demands on the type of equipment and the exposure settings you use. You need to get to understand intuitively how much depth of field you need in any situation — and how to get it with the lens you are using. This can be done only through lots of practice, but understanding what is going on inside your lens helps.

Aviation photographers habitually use long lenses, and they use fast shutter speeds to freeze action and avoid blurring. These both suggest wide apertures Yet, as accurate focus is so important, a small stop, giving plenty of depth of field would be useful. We'll examine this in more detail when we come to exposure, but it's as well to be aware of this dilemma straight away.

As there are such contradictory aperture requirements, it's a good idea to get your focusing right in the first place — then there will be less need for depth of field. As we are mainly

If the background is interesting, use it. This is sometimes a better option than getting closer

Opposite: Use details like smoke to fill the frame

worried about moving subjects, there are two main techniques: pull focus and pre-focus.

Pull focus is where you constantly change the focus as the subject moves away from or towards you. It can be a tricky skill to master, which is why you find specialist 'focus pullers' in the movie business. With cine film or video, focus has to be pulled to keep the image sharp throughout the shot, but the technique is just as useful in stills work.

You start by focusing on the subject well before it has got to the position where you want to shoot it. If the subject is an aircraft coming down the display line, for example, you would focus on it when it is still well off to one side. You then keep the subject in the frame making a continuous and smooth correction to the focus until it is in position at which time you shoot.

It sounds difficult, but with a little practice you can easily become fluent. The speed of the aircraft is unlikely to change suddenly, and you will find yourself being able to predict the speed of the focus shift fairly accurately without having to think about it.

The alternative is to focus the lens on the spot where you want the aircraft to be when you shoot it, and wait for the aircraft to reach that point. This is pre-focusing, and might at first seem the preferred option. If you have the same aircraft coming to the same spot time and time again, it can be an effective technique. The problem arises when you photograph the aircraft for the first time. You are likely to find that when the aircraft reaches the assigned spot, it is still tiny in the frame, or you might realise before it gets there that it is going to be too big. Either way you are left changing your aim to another point,

On static taildraggers, watch out for sloping horizons. Lining up the aircraft in the frame means you may be tempted to make the aircraft level and the horizon slanted

scrabbling around with the focus to salvage the shot.

The other major problem is being able to recognise the spot when the aircraft gets there. You could leave the camera, perhaps mounted on a tripod, aimed at the location, and shoot when the aircraft comes into frame. The trouble with aeroplanes, however, is that they are rarely so obliging. The odds are that it will be slightly too high or low, or will change its track a little so that it doesn't pass through the pre-focused point at all. What's more, you need lightning sharp reactions to take shots in that way if you aren't going to end up with just a nose or tail.

This is not to say that pre-focusing is out entirely. You can use a combination of the two. For instance, if you know that the aircraft is likely to make its pass directly over the runway, focus the lens on the runway before it arrives. Now hold the focusing ring so that a thumb or finger is at a position that can be easily remembered — the six o'clock position is the best. Now track the aircraft using the pull focus technique. When your finger is in the six o'clock position you know that the aircraft will be nearly in focus, but you can still make minor adjustments easily, having followed the aeroplane on its run in.

Pre-focusing is much easier if the aircraft is moving across your field of vision. Although its distance from you is constantly changing, the rate of change is much less than when it is coming towards you or moving away from you. With this kind of lateral movement, pre-focusing with a little adjustment at the moment of shooting, is a viable technique.

Some long lenses, especially fast telephotos, have pre-focus collars. A ring can be set so that the focus clicks into place at a predetermined spot. This can be useful for the type of technique we've just discussed.

It also helps to keep both eyes open, even when one is pressed to the viewfinder. This is something which needs practice, and not everyone feels comfortable doing it, but it does make you more aware of what is going on around you.

Regardless of whether you pre-focus or pull focus, you should always track the aircraft through the lens. This not only increases your chances of it still being in the frame when you trip the shutter, it also helps keep the image sharp, as we will see.

As we mentioned in the section on equipment, autofocus systems can be a liability in this kind of work. Even those capable of changing focus quickly enough are prone to being fooled by bright reflections and areas of shadow. And because the angle of view of the system is very small — reading just a tiny rectangle in the centre of the viewfinder — if the subject isn't kept bang in the middle of the frame your shot is likely to end up blurred. This is both difficult and a severe limitation on your creativity.

That said, autofocus systems do have their place in aviation work. If the subject is likely to be large in the frame, virtually or actually filling it, those latter objections disappear. And there are some intriguing benefits. For example, some systems offer an interesting variation on prefocusing, in that they are capable of tripping the shutter when the image comes into focus.

If you consistently have trouble with manual focusing, it's worth exploring autofocus systems. But one word of caution — take care when using them for air-to-air shots. Grimy windows can fool the system into thinking that you want a shot of the window itself, rather than the scene outside.

Even if you don't have autofocus, your camera is probably fitted with some focus aids. Split image rangefinders, in the centre of the focusing screen, use two opposite-sloping prisms. With an out-of-focus image, they bend the light in slightly different directions, thus splitting the image along the boundary

Watch out for bits of other aircraft ruining the outline of your subject. This can be avoided by moving to a different vantage point or going for a detail shot

where they meet. This system is easy to use so long as you have something like a straight edge, where the split can be clearly seen. Incidentally, if the split is horizontal and the only straight edge you have in the image is also horizontal, you can always turn the camera through 90 degrees, just for focusing. It's a simple point, but one often missed. Some cameras have the split set at 45 degrees to the horizontal to improve the chances of finding a suitable edge.

As an alternative to a split image rangefinder — or more often these days as a ring around it — many cameras are fitted with a microprism system. This works on a similar principle, but instead uses hundreds of tiny pyramids which scatter the light when it is out-of-focus. Microprisms vary from the moderately useful to the hopeless.

Both systems share one common fault, which is that they stop working as soon as the lens aperture gets down to around $f5.6$. That means they are hopeless with long lenses, which is when you most need them.

If you are able to change the screen in your camera, as you can with most professional systems, a plain, ground glass screen is worth considering. The focusing devices can be more of a distraction than an aid, tempting you to fiddle around too long, with the usual danger of missing the shot. A plain screen gives an uncluttered view, and with practice is just as accurate. Many professionals use a ground glass screen etched with a fine grid. This helps line up horizontal and vertical lines, which is handy if you have problems with your horizons.

WHAT TO FOCUS ON

Assuming that you are still focusing the old fashioned way, what do you focus on? Too many people make the mistake of turning the focus ring until the overall image looks generally sharp. It is far better to decide on one small detail in the scene — preferably something with nice crisp, well-defined edges — which you want to make sure is sharp. It should be the most important part. With aircraft, it is likely to be the cockpit. Put all your effort into making that sharp, using depth of field to take care of the rest.

With a static subject, where you have plenty of time, there is one technique which can help you to decide where to focus and how much depth of field you need. First, you choose the closest point which you want to have in focus. This might be the nose of the aeroplane. Focus on that point, and then take a look at the focusing ring of the lens. Note the distance indicated by the focus index scale — in other words, the distance from the lens to the nose. You might like to make a small mark on the focus scale with a chinagraph pencil.

Next, decide on the furthest point which should be sharp — the tail, perhaps. Repeat the procedure with this. You will now have two marks on the focus scale, the distance between them

You don't just use different focal lengths to fill the frame at different distances. Even when you stay put, having a choice of focal lengths is useful, to create different compositions

representing the depth of field you need for that shot. Now you use the depth of field index marks on the lens. Turn the lens focus ring until the two marks you made line up with, or fall inside, the two marks for one aperture. By shooting at that aperture you will know that everything from the nose to the tail will be sharp. Just for good measure, you might like to go one stop down — if the chinagraph marks line up with the ƒ8 index lines, for example, you would probably want to shoot at ƒ11 just to be sure.

There is one other technique which is more useful in situations where you have to work quickly, and it's based on a value known as the hyperfocal distance. This is the point where the depth of field just about extends to infinity, from a point half-way between you and the focus point. If you focus any closer, infinity will not be sharp. If you focus further away, the closest point made sharp by depth of field also moves away. So using the hyperfocal distance gives you the maximum depth of field for any given lens and aperture — pocket and compact cameras with fixed-focus lenses use this technique.

The hyperfocal distance is most useful with wide angle lenses. With a 24 mm lens set to ƒ8, the hyperfocal distance — the distance you should set at the normal focus index — is 2.18 metres. At those settings, everything from 1.09 metres to infinity will be sharp! That's why news photographers often use hyperfocal distance to preset lenses for grab shots. With a 300 mm lens at the same stop, the nearest point in focus is 46.33 metres away, with the hyperfocal distance at 92.67 metres — not quite so useful.

To set the hyperfocal distance on your lens, move the focus ring until the infinity mark coincides with the depth of field index mark for the aperture in use. As a guide, some hyperfocal distances for different lenses at different stops are given in the following table. Remember that these are the distances you set against the normal focus index. The nearest points in focus are half these distances. The numbers have been rounded up — it's always best to be a bit pessimistic.

Lens	20 mm	24 mm	35 mm	50 mm	85 mm
Stop					
ƒ2.8	5	6.5	14	28	79
ƒ4	3.5	4.5	9.5	19	55
ƒ5.6	2.5	3.5	7	14	40
ƒ8	2	2.5	5	10	28
ƒ11	1.5	2	3.5	7	20
ƒ16	1	1.5	2.5	5	7

It's viewpoint that affects perspective. These three shots of a KC-130F show the effect of moving closer using progressively wider lenses

One final note, which is connected with focusing to some extent, is that you shouldn't shoot just because the subject is in focus. There is a distinct tendency, even among those photographers who should know better, to hit the trigger as soon as the shot looks reasonable. All too often, the aircraft is a tiny dot in an ocean of sky when the picture is developed. The subject always seems closer and looks larger than it really is, so it's worth trying to develop an awareness of the edges of the frame and how much your subject is filling it. That's not to say that you should refrain from shooting until the frame is filled: you could miss a lot of shots that way. But you can avoid a lot of wasted film if you can resist the urge to shoot as soon as you have the aircraft in your sights.

Another point allied to that, and which may seem a little contradictory, is that it is often best to shoot even though the shot isn't perfect: you can always loose off another frame if the picture improves. It's all very well waiting for the aircraft to fly into the perfect position: but if it doesn't, and you haven't taken any shots, then the picture is missed entirely even though you would have accepted a slightly less than perfect shot. The same applies even to static aircraft. If you can't seem to get rid of the crowds, or general tat surrounding the aircraft, take the picture anyway. At least that way you have some kind of picture in the bag. Then, if matters improve later — perhaps only a split second later — you can get the shot you wanted. Motor-drives are helpful in this context if the situation is changing rapidly.

If you have a lot of foreground to fill — a common problem with wide angle lenses — try using the aircraft's shadow

GETTING IT STEADY

Sharpness is not just about focusing. You can get the focus racked out to perfect precision and still wind up with a blurred shot simply because you have moved the camera during the exposure.

Camera shake is not properly understood by most people, yet it ruins as many pictures as poor focus. The two effects can be easily confused when you are looking at the final result. If there is *something* sharp in the picture (even if it's not your main subject), or if the degree of blurring varies with subject distance in the same frame, then your problem is probably inaccurate focusing. Sometimes camera shake will manifest itself as a slight blurring of the whole picture but in only one direction. Take a look at the edges of the objects. If they are smudged along the top and bottom edges (the most common direction of the fault) but not at the sides, the chances are that you've suffered camera shake. Just as often, however, the problem is a general blurring of the image, and so you may be not aware that you are suffering a case of the shakes, and may be blaming it on focusing inadequacies.

Camera shake and focusing errors do have something in common: they become more of a problem the more you enlarge the image. If you never intend to have anything larger than postcard-size prints, then you may be able to live with a little fuzziness. However, if you want bigger prints, or want to project or sell your pictures, then absolute sharpness is essential.

This is especially true with aviation work for a couple of reasons. Any kind of blurring destroys fine detail, and it is precisely that kind of detail which is essential in aeroplane pictures — you really do want to see the registration numbers, the small design variations, the minutiae of markings

Sometimes the shadows can be dramatic enough to become the main element of the picture

and construction, even the smile on the pilot's face. In addition, the constraints imposed by the subject mean that it's not uncommon to have to blow up or use just a section of the image because you didn't have a long enough lens or couldn't get sufficiently close to the subject. So you have to start with a really sharp image to cope with the extra enlargement to make the aircraft large enough in the final print.

The problem is made worse by long lenses, which magnify any camera movement. Most books tell you that a tripod is essential with lenses of more than 200 mm focal length. As we will see, this is untrue and positively unhelpful in aviation work.

It's a popular misconception that a lightweight camera is better for avoiding camera shake. Assuming that the equipment isn't too heavy that your arm begins to tremble, you are better off with something with some weight behind it. That's because the extra mass adds momentum, and there is less tendency for the camera and your hands to flutter about at the slightest twitch. This is yet another benefit of the motordrive. Packed with heavy batteries and mounted inside a strong metal body, the average motordrive adds weight, bulk and — usually — a more substantial grip.

There are various kinds of physical support which can help, but they usually impose their own problems. This is another example of where aviation practice runs contrary to common photographic wisdom. What this means in this case is that tripods are out — well, nearly.

Trying to track a moving aircraft with a camera mounted on a tripod will bring you nothing but grief. If the tripod head is not to slow down the movement of the camera, all the locks have to be left very loose, thus sacrificing most of the benefits of having the tripod in the first place. Even so, you will find yourself unable to move the camera with sufficient freedom.

Obviously, the same is not true of a static subject, and a tripod can be of some benefit here, especially when shooting in low light — in a hangar or museum, for example. Poor light invariably means longer exposure times, which in turn leads to more camera shake. Whenever the speed goes below 1/30th, sticking the camera on some kind of solid support is a wise move. And that brings us to an important point about tripods: there is little point in spending good money on lightweight tripods. The small, channel-legged items that are so common these days give you little advantage over hand-holding. They have to be big and heavy to be worth using. That's one reason why outdoors, in reasonable daylight, you're better off without the extra bulk and weight of the three-legged beast.

Aircraft moving at different speeds create different amounts of blur, even when one is kept sharp by panning

The biggest problem with a tripod is that it has too many legs. The very thing that makes it useful — its static solidity — makes it an inflexible liability for any kind of action work. A potentially useful halfway house between the tripod and hand-holding is the monopod, essentially a tripod with one leg.

Naturally, the monopod is a good deal lighter than the tripod and allows you to pan quite freely by twisting the leg. Sports photographers use them a great deal. However, people shooting athletics, football or even motor racing have one major advantage over aviation photographers — their subjects, for the most part, stay on the ground, roughly at the same level as the photographer.

Aeroplanes are not so accommodating. When you track an aircraft flying past, your line of sight describes an arc through the air. The closer the aircraft comes to your position, the more pronounced the arc. Although a monopod allows free movement sideways, it is still restricting vertically. With the height of the monopod locked for convenient shooting of an aircraft some distance away, you will find that when that aircraft gets closer you have to lift the camera higher. The result is a monopod waving around in the air instead of being firmly planted on the ground, making matters worse instead of better.

With aircraft that never get very close, the monopod can work well, especially with long lenses. It can also prove useful to help sharpen up pictures of static subjects, and as most monopods are reasonably light they are less of a hassle to carry around than tripods.

If you do find yourself using a tripod or monopod you will invariably find yourself in a situation where you need to get the camera off the support quickly, for a snatch shot. Fast release attachments, which have one part that fits on the camera and another that goes on the tripod or monopod, are useful for quick switching.

Pistol grips, which screw into the tripod socket on the camera or lens and provide a cable release for tripping the shutter, are of dubious benefit. Most modern cameras give you a reasonable grip. All a pistol grip does is take your hand away from where it is most needed — near the controls. The cable release may be able to trip the shutter once, but on most cameras is incapable of properly operating motordrives.

Rifle grips are a little better, in that they provide good stability with long lenses. But they suffer from the same drawbacks as pistol grips. They can also cause a few heart-stopping moments around military or security-conscious installations if they are mistaken for the real thing!

Finally, a mini- or table-top tripod, fixed to the camera and balanced on your chest, will provide some support. It may give you a sore neck or a temporary stoop, but in the absence of anything else, it's worth a try. Ultimately, however, you are much better off learning to hold the camera and lens properly.

Keeping the camera still makes ground subjects sharp but the aircraft is blurred

TECHNIQUES

There is something of an art to holding a camera, and it is one which has to be mastered if you are going to deal with an action subject like flying aircraft. Before you start throwing the camera around, trying to catch elusive aeroplanes, you have to learn to hold it steady enough to avoid camera shake.

Holding the camera in both hands is just about acceptable if the lens is fairly short. But with any kind of long lens, the centre of gravity is further forward, and that type of grip is not so stable. You need one hand on the camera and one on the lens. Indeed, as you are dealing with fast-moving subjects anyway, you will need your fingers constantly on the focusing ring.

One piece of conventional wisdom which *is* worth remembering is: Don't Jab The Shutter Button. This is a frequent cause of camera shake as the direction of the force you are applying is across the frame, perpendicular to the direction of the light forming the image. Some camera manufacturers have tried to solve this problem by mounting the shutter release on the front of the camera, so that the pressure is along the lens axis. But most of us are stuck with the conventional top-mounted release. Modern cameras and most motordrives, which have electronic releases, are better in that they require only a slight pressure to release the shutter. But whatever camera you have, the advice is the same: squeeze on the pressure in a smooth fluid motion, the same way you should pull the trigger of a gun. If you are using a small camera, put your thumb on the bottom of the casing and your forefinger on the release and squeeze both towards each other — the two pressures in opposite directions should cancel out any camera movement.

Even the way you stand can affect sharpness. We've all watched scenes on TV where a cop assumes a firing position. Well, photographers can benefit from doing something similar, especially when using long lenses hand-held. The best stance is with your feet about 18 inches apart, one slightly in front of the other, leaving the body well-balanced. This way you are able to twist freely to pan with the action. Give yourself the maximum freedom to follow unpredictable aircraft.

FAST SHUTTER SPEED

The easiest way to minimize camera shake is to select a fast shutter speed. Camera movement or vibration can still affect the sharpness of the image even at speeds of 1/500th or 1/1000th, but it is less likely. When in doubt, go to a faster speed.

It is often said that the fastest speed you should ever use is the reciprocal of the lens' focal length. In other words, if you are using a 200 mm lens, you should use speeds of around 1/200th and faster. This is nonsense — or at least impractical. With practice you should be able to use much slower speeds than this, although if the subject is moving you will need higher speeds anyway.

Fast shutter speeds will also help overcome blurring caused by another problem — subject movement. This is where the subject moves during the time that the shutter is open, and can happen quite easily with aircraft. In fact, aircraft can be so fast that using a short exposure is simply not enough to ensure sharp pictures.

Panning the camera with the aircraft keeps the subject sharp while the background blurs

The best known and most successful remedy is to move the camera with the subject — a technique known as panning. If you keep the subject in the same place in the frame it won't blur. The background, which is now travelling rapidly across the frame, probably will blur, but that just gives a quite appropriate impression of speed and can be used to get rid of distracting background details. Indeed, photographers who have mastered the skills of panning deliberately select quite slow shutter speeds — 1/60th or even slower — to accentuate the background blurring.

Achieving a smooth pan is tricky at first, but only a little practice is needed for most people to become proficient. It helps if there is something in the centre of the focusing screen — a focus aid, autofocus reference point, even cross hairs — which you can use to lock on to a part of the aircraft. But it is equally important to be aware of what is outside the frame: you don't want to pan perfectly only to have a telegraph pole, parked aircraft or other obstruction leap into the frame just at the moment you hit the button. And it is easy to pan straight into the sun. Either way, if you do get the shot it probably isn't worth having, so be aware of what is around you, and where the sun is.

The effects of speed blur are more pronounced when the subject is travelling laterally across the frame. A head-on shot of an aircraft coming straight at you is unlikely to suffer subject blur as it isn't moving across the frame at all. So the more acute the angle of attack between your line of sight and the aircraft's flight path, the less you will suffer subject blur. Of course, with a head-on shot you swap one problem for another, as you now have to pull focus very deftly to keep the image sharp — a skill which is even tougher to master than panning. And this is precisely the kind of situation where autofocus systems put up their hands and surrender.

There is an effect which comes into play called angular velocity. Let's assume the aircraft is on a straight track, which will take it past you. When it is some distance away, it appears to be moving slowly. The angle through which you have to pan the camera to keep up with it during, say, one second is very small. When it is close, even though its airspeed hasn't changed, you are having to pan much faster to keep up with it — the angular velocity is faster. One of the results is that, although you may pan at the right speed to

In low light with shutter speeds longer than 1/15th even accurate panning might not be enough to make the aircraft completely sharp, but the results can still be effective

keep the front of the aircraft sharp, because the back is at a different distance, and therefore has a different angular velocity, it may be blurred!

Panning does create two potential pitfalls, both connected with changing light conditions as you rapidly change your direction of view. First, if the subject in the frame changes quickly from being a generally bright subject — sunlit skies and bright reflections, that kind of thing — to a generally dark subject, the meter in your camera may not be able to keep up with the pace. Like many instruments, there is a slight delay as the meter gets used to the new light level. Normally, this wouldn't matter, but everything happens so fast when you're panning that it can result in wrong exposure when you're shooting on automatic. In our example — moving from bright to dark subjects — the shot would be under-exposed. And the opposite is true, too; moving from dark to bright could lead to over-exposure. Using manual exposure is the only real solution, although it should be noted that modern camera systems suffer far less from this sort of delay.

The second problem is simpler. When you're busy concentrating on the aircraft, it's easy to forget about where you're pointing the camera. You may be following the subject perfectly, keeping the pan exactly right, when suddenly . . . zap! Instead of a beautifully framed aircraft cruising in azure skies, you have an eyeful of dazzling sunlight, a silhouetted aircraft and an over-exposed photograph. Even if the problem isn't as drastic as panning into the sun, you can find awkward and ugly subjects creeping into the frame. If you're lucky they will be blurred or out of focus, but there are eternal laws which state that they'll be perfectly sharp and obvious. Knowing what's around you is the only solution — and some luck helps.

Panning from a brightly-lit part of the sky into shadows can result in under-exposure on auto systems, which often have a slight response lag

Finally, when it comes to getting things sharp, there's also a case for carefully choosing the right moment. For example, if an aircraft performing aerobatics starts into a vertical climb, there's a good chance it will perform a stall or hammerhead turn, or some other manoeuvre in which the machine is practically stationary. That's the time to shoot. Sports photographers use a similar technique — waiting for the ball to reach the top of its bounce, or an athlete to reach the top of the jump.

There may be times — such as when the light is starting to go at the end of a display — when you simply can't get a fast enough shutter speed to ensure sharpness. This is the time to try a bit of creativity and blur for effect. With a slow shutter speed and fast panning you can get dramatic shots with not a single sharp bit in them. You don't want to do it too often, of course, but it's fun to try.

EXPOSURE

One day we will get to the point where worrying about exposure is a thing of the past. And we really haven't got very far to go. The exposure systems you find built into today's cameras are closer to miniature computers than the old light-cell-and-needle jobs of

A wide angle shot of the whole aircraft sometimes means unavoidable clutter. Selecting a detail with a long lens can avoid this

yesteryear. Even so, no system is perfect. There are situations which the best systems find difficult — a small, dark aeroplane against a big, bright sky being a classic example — and in any case, exposure is another creative step, a process which you can manipulate for aesthetic as well as technical reasons, and one which needs to be exercised with some care and finesse.

Let's define some terms here. The word 'exposure' describes how much light energy reaches any particular piece of film. It thus depends on three factors: the amount of light radiated or reflected by the subject; the amount of light transmitted by the lens; and the time for which this light is allowed to fall on the film. Sometimes you will come across terms such as 'an exposure of 1/250th': this isn't strictly accurate, but being colloquial usage we'll let it pass.

The main thing to note is that the two factors which are always within your control — exposure time (through control of the shutter speed) and light transmission through the lens (by selecting the aperture) have a direct link. For any given scene, increasing the exposure time means decreasing the light transmission, or in practical terms, selecting a longer shutter speed means using a smaller aperture — and vice versa. If you supply the light yourself, in the form of flash or other kinds of artificial lighting, this increases your options a little.

It is possible to set your camera and lens using the recommendations printed on the box or leaflet that came with the film. And on sunny days, you could try using the old 'sunny 16' rule, where you select $f16$ and a shutter speed which is the nearest you can get to the reciprocal of the film speed: if the film is ISO 100 you would use 1/125th. And who knows? You might even get away with it. But the results are unlikely to be perfect.

Too slow a shutter speed leads to subject blur and camera shake, particularly when tracking fast moving subjects

You are more likely to be using the metering system built into your camera. This is, in the vast majority of cases, a TTL system, in that it reads the light coming 'through the lens'. And more often than not, these days, it will be feeding its information directly to some sort of automatic exposure system.

There is no one 'correct' exposure for any scene, in spite of what your light meter might tell you. A meter will give you an exposure value for the current lighting conditions on the basis that the subject contains a standard distribution of tones, as we'll see in a minute. But, even assuming you don't want to modify the exposure for any reason, that value can be met with a variety of shutter speed and aperture combinations.

Given a certain light level and speed of film, the correct exposure — according to the meter — might be 1/125th at $f8$. If you want to shoot at $f5.6$ instead, which is one stop more light through the lens, then you can keep the exposure correct by giving a shorter exposure time by the same amount — one stop. In this case it would mean using 1/250th. Similarly, 1/60th at $f11$, 1/30th at $f16$ and 1/500th at $f4$ all give the same exposure, and we could go on with more combinations.

If all the combinations give the same exposure value, does it matter which one we use? Well, the answer is yes — very much so. Indeed, the selection of the correct aperture and shutter speed settings can be the most important decisions you make. Before we get on to that, however, let's look at the business of meter readings.

Most exposure metering systems are based on the principle of 'averaging' out the tones in a picture. Imagine that the image is made from fine sand in various grey tints from black to white (we'll think in terms of monochrome to avoid confusing the issue with colour, as we are talking about simple light levels, or tonal values). The theory is that, in a 'typical' scene, if you were to mix all the sand evenly together it would come out as a standard mid-grey.

It is this assumption that every scene contains an even distribution of tones which can trip up some metering systems. Let's assume you are taking a picture of a flat piece of mid-grey card. The metering system will be perfectly happy with this and will give you an exposure which will reproduce the card as mid-grey in the final picture. If you then replace the card with another piece — this time white — the system assumes the scene is still mid-grey (because it *always* does) and attributes the extra brilliance to an increase in the general light level. The result is that it gives less exposure so that the card still comes out as mid-grey in the picture. A similar thing happens with a black card, but this time more exposure is given to bring it up to mid-grey.

An aircraft half in and half out of the shadows presents a tricky metering situation. It's usually best to expose for the highlights, but bracketing is recommended

These are extreme cases, but they demonstrate the principle: scenes which contain large areas of light tones will tend to be under-exposed, while those with large dark areas will be over-exposed. In the case of pictures of cards, this probably wouldn't matter — there is only one tone in each picture, albeit inaccurately reproduced in the case of the white and black cards.

However, if you introduce another element into the shot, this exposure inaccuracy can become critical. Your large, bright expanse could be the sky and the extra element an aircraft flying through it. As the sky dominates the shot, the exposure is reduced with the result that the aircraft, which wasn't big enough to have much

of an effect on the exposure system, comes out as an under-exposed silhouette.

And size is not the only factor. The bright subject can be very small and still confuse the meter. Aircraft often have shiny paint schemes which efficiently reflect light, almost like mirrors. Canopies do this too. The result is that the sun, or artificial lights show up as small hotspots of light, and these can be so much brighter than the aircraft itself that they affect the meter reading, once again leading to under-exposure.

Over-exposure is not quite so common, but it happens. Aircraft with dark paint schemes can be a problem if they are large in the frame. The meter system sees the dark tones and assumes that there isn't much light around. The exposure it suggests will reproduce the paint scheme as mid-grey, but any surrounding subjects, such as the sky and landscape, are likely to be over-exposed.

In recent years, camera manufacturers have tried to solve these sorts of problems with 'multi-pattern' metering systems — pioneered by Nikon in the FA camera. Rather than read the whole scene with one meter cell, these systems read five or so separate areas — usually dividing the frame into quarters, reading each separately, and then reading the centre with another cell to provide 'centre-weighting'. The general light level is calculated, but more importantly, the distribution of light levels is compared with an internal database which the manufacturers derived from studying tens of thousands of pictures. In this way, the system can recognise non-standard scenes and correct the exposure accordingly. And it works very well, giving excellent exposure in something like ninety-five per cent of cases. But . . . the other five per cent of shots probably contain aeroplanes!

Deliberate slight under-exposure can be used to hide an unattractive background, if it's in the shadows

Hand-held meters are more or less prone to these errors, depending on the way you use them. In 'reflected light' mode, you point the meter at the subject you want to shoot and measure the light coming from it. This method suffers all the problems of TTL metering, with one extra drawback — the TTL system measures only the scene which appears in the picture, whereas a hand-held meter covers a wider area.

A more accurate way of using the meter is to measure the amount of light falling on to the subject, rather than coming from it. This is known as 'incident' light metering, and is used a great deal by studio photographers. As you are ignoring the subject, its colour and tonal values cannot affect the reading, which is why incident metering is usually very accurate.

There are two ways of doing this. The awkward method is to take a direct meter reading from a special photographic grey card (which represents the 'standard' mid-grey). The more sensible technique is to use a light meter which can take an incident dome — a hemispherical diffuser which fits over the light cell. The meter is held near the subject, pointing at the camera, although if you can't get near the aeroplane, and you are sure you are being lit by the same light as the subject, holding the meter at arm's length, again pointing towards the camera, will do.

Incident readings still have to be used with a little care — a very dark subject, such as a black-painted SR-71 or an olive drab fighter, may *have* to be given a little more exposure — usually about a stop — to prevent it becoming one big featureless blob. And incident readings can be tricky if they are taken in the shadow of a cloud while your subject is in sunshine, or vice versa. Indeed, the TTL meter is still best for moving subjects, which constantly change their inclination to the sun. But for stationary objects the incident reading is useful.

Why bother about correct exposure? Well, film is not as adaptable as the eye. When you look at a scene, you scan bits at a time, and as you do so, the aperture in your eye, the pupil, changes size to accommodate different light levels. It may take a short time to adapt to large changes, which is why you are

Below (left): A classic exposure problem — a light subject on a dark background will fool an exposure meter into thinking the subject is generally dark. Here the auto exposure system has been overridden to prevent over-exposure of the aircraft. (Right): The opposite of the previous problem — a dark subject on a large, bright background can result in the aircraft being reduced to an under-exposed silhouette

sometimes dazzled by bright lights and stumble around blind when you walk from sunshine into a dark room. But in normal scenes, there is no problem.

Film is not so smart. On the whole, a given exposure on a piece of film produces a given tone. If the light level increases, and the shutter and aperture settings stay the same, then the tone will get brighter until the film can no longer cope. If you think about a negative, bright subject tones are represented by black image tones. But there is a limit to how dense the black bits can be, and this limit might be reached sooner than you think. Objects which the eye can discern as a surface with some tonal values become plain white in the picture. They are, in photographic terms, 'burnt out'. Similarly, the deepest black an image can handle is represented by an almost clear piece of film in the negative (there is some residual tone called 'base fog' caused, not by exposure, but by the processing).

The ability of film to cope with a range of tones varies with the type of emulsion. If you take your meter reading from a mid-grey tone and set the exposure accordingly, the film may still be able to record reasonable detail in areas up to four stops brighter and five stops darker than the mid-tone. This gives a total brightness range of nine stops. As each stop represents a doubling of the light level, the brightest recordable area is thus 512 times brighter than the darkest. On a sunny day, the brightness range might be 500:1, so you can see that our exposure would cope with this, providing it was right in the first place.

If a picture is incorrectly exposed, areas of the subject in the mid-tone range may appear, although with the wrong tones. But with over-exposure, brighter areas will go above the upper threshold, becoming featureless, burnt-out white tones. You will also lose fine details, including struts and bracing wires on biplanes, and even complete glass canopies. The worst problems occur when the subject is backlit, by direct sun or a bright, slightly overcast sky. In under-exposure, darker tones disappear into featureless shadows. And there is nothing you can do to restore this detail once it has gone.

Some photographers talk about 'exposure latitude' as if it is some kind of great safety net for people with lousy exposure technique. But exposure latitude is badly misunderstood. All too often it is interpreted as being the extent to which you can get the exposure 'wrong' and still get a perfect result. In fact, it means that you can use a range of exposures and still get reasonable detail in both highlights and shadow areas, which is significantly different.

Note that we are talking about detail, not tonal values. Latitude is really of interest only to people taking shots on negative films. With transparency films, you choose the tones which will represent your subject at the time you shoot. With negative films, this is done at the printing stage, and you can correct for some inaccuracy in exposure. So long as the fault is within limits, and the brightness range of the subject not too extreme, you won't have lost highlight or shadow details. But this latitude can be smaller than you might think — perhaps only a stop or two.

So we've seen why correct exposure is important. A bit later we'll discuss why you might not want to trust your light meter. But first, let's think about the settings you might want to use.

CHOOSING THE APERTURE

Apart from its effect on exposure, the main reason for altering the aperture is to control depth of field. The smaller the stop (the larger the f-number) the more depth you have.

If the subject is moving, getting the focus absolutely right can be tricky, especially with long lenses. Even the best autofocus systems can get a little hot and bothered when faced with an aircraft coming head-on at 500 mph. The more depth you have, the less this matters, as small inaccuracies will be covered up, although you still can't afford to be complacent.

Having some extra depth also helps if the main subject isn't alone. If there are two or more aeroplanes in the shot, you first have to decide which one to focus on (normally the closest) and then let depth of field bring the other into focus. The same is true if you want background details, such as the landscape, sharp along with the aircraft. With the longer lenses, you might need a fair bit of depth just to get all of one aircraft sharp. If you focus on the canopy, the tail could be blurred, if you haven't stopped down enough.

Limited depth of field throws the background out of focus, though it's still sharp enough in this case to play a part in the composition

With long lenses — 200 mm or more — apertures of $f11$ or smaller should cover most minor focusing errors. If you want to get more than one aircraft, going down to $f16$ certainly helps. Shorter lenses, which have greater depth of field anyway, can be used with wider apertures. By the time you're down to a 35 mm, an aperture of $f5.6$ will cover most eventualities. But bear in mind that the more depth of field you have, the greater your insurance against unsharp pictures.

Massive depth of field isn't always an advantage. There are occasions when the only thing you want to be sharp is the main subject. The most common example of this in aviation photography is when you are shooting a static subject and want to throw irrelevant details in the background — chimneys, fences and that kind of thing — out-of-focus.

This selective depth of field, also known as selective or differential focus, can be highly effective. To use it accurately, however, you have to be aware of how the lens will behave. A depth of field preview button on the camera — which stops the lens down to its preselected aperture — is certainly helpful here. And you can take a look at the depth of field scale on the lens as a rough guide (see the section on focusing). Long lenses, with their small depth of field, are most useful for this kind of effect.

93

Indeed, getting selective focus with the wider wide angles is almost impossible.

Sometimes, you may be tempted to rack the lens wide open to get the fastest shutter speed possible. It seems that people are more worried about camera shake than focusing errors. However, aside from the fact that you will leave yourself with an uncomfortably shallow depth of field, in which some parts of the aircraft may be blurred even when others are sharp, you are not getting the most out of your lenses.

Most optics reach their optimum resolution when shut down two or three stops from the maximum. The improvement is particularly noticeable at the edges of the frame. Further stopping down has little effect, and may start to degrade sharpness a little once you get to values like $f16$. Every bit of sharpness you can muster is worth having, so turning an $f2.8$ lens to $f5.6$ or $f8$ is a good idea.

CHOOSING THE SHUTTER SPEED

The choice of shutter speed is, if anything, more critical than the aperture, especially if your subject is moving. The length of time for which the film is exposed will determine how much the subject blurs, as its image moves across the film, and how much the picture is blurred by the camera itself moving.

In the case of an aeroplane hurtling across the sky, you will want to use a fast shutter speed to minimize blurring — to 'freeze' the subject. By a happy coincidence, this is compatible with selecting a shutter speed to avoid camera shake, which is always more noticeable with the kind of long lens you are likely to be using.

Even if your hand is rock steady, you might still suffer from the shakes if you are in an aircraft yourself. In air-to-air photography, aircraft vibration is an underestimated evil. And the only way to be rid of it is to use fast shutter speeds.

As with depth of field, a little extra insurance is always worthwhile. So, even when you suspect that a speed of 1/250th is likely to be fast enough to solve all your problems (which is probably true), going to 1/500th, 1/1000th or even faster will give you greater peace of mind. If you are using a camera strapped to an aircraft, the higher speeds are almost mandatory.

However, there can be an unwanted side-effect from using fast shutter speeds. When the subject is propeller driven, a fast speed is quite capable of freezing the prop blades, which looks unnatural and even ugly. You might even leave viewers with the impression that they are looking at a photograph of a model, which can be galling when you've gone through hell to get the shot.

Propellers might look as though they are moving fast, but the camera knows different. Speeds of 1/1000th or faster are capable of freezing the blades completely, while even 1/500th will often reduce them to spindly-looking sticks, instead of the savage

Deep focus helps to get all the parts of the picture sharp

meat-slicers we know them to be. You really need a reasonable amount of blur for props to look attractive.

It is difficult to give a hard-and-fast rule about which shutter speed to use. The speed of the propeller itself will vary depending on the type of aircraft and what the pilot is doing at the time.

A slow enough speed will result in the props creating a complete disc on the image, but it is often nice to know how many blades the prop has, and so the best results are often obtained when each blade is discernible, but blurred. Take a three-bladed prop, for example. If it is moving at 2,000 revolutions per minute (rpm), a shutter speed of 1/250th will allow each blade to move through an angle of approximately 48 degrees, which will look quite attractive. Moving up one speed, to 1/500th, will give a blurring of only 24 degrees, which will start to look a little weedy.

Some aircraft, including race machines and aerobatic types, use higher revs than this, while turbo-props are often surprisingly slow. The problem, of course, is knowing how fast the prop is going. It's hardly a simple matter of asking the pilot! This is where research pays off — although practice and trial and error are equally rewarding. If, while the aircraft is on the ground, you can get to the pilot or crew of the subject aircraft, or a similar type, then you can ask. Otherwise it's a case of scanning the reference books beforehand if you know you are going to photograph a specific aircraft. As a rough rule of thumb, however, speeds of 1/125th and 1/250th (in that order) give the best results with props.

It is hard to think of instances when you might want to go the other way. It is possible to produce interesting images by deliberately blurring the subject, so long as you blur it enough! But few people will want to do that with aircraft.

The only other possible reason for using a deliberately slow shutter speed is to get rid of people! If a static display of some kind is constantly surrounded by onlookers, you can sometimes make them insignificant by making them blurred. When people move during a long exposure, they become faint, blurred streaks, and may even disappear altogether. You will need an exposure of at least one second, and perhaps as much as five or ten seconds, so the technique is most useful in museums, where low light levels allow this kind of thing. People positioned directly between the camera and the subject can still be a problem, and there is always someone who manages to stay still for the wrong ten seconds.

Different shutter speeds create different amounts of blurring of a spinning prop. These shots were taken at 1/60th, 1/125th and 1/250th of a second

RECIPROCITY LAW FAILURE

The direct trade-off between shutter speed and aperture is simple enough most of the time. But if stopping down the lens, or shooting in dim conditions means that the exposure time gets down to around a second or more, you hit a problem commonly known as *reciprocity failure* — but more precisely called reciprocity *law* failure.

It is easy to believe that increases or decreases of light level can be compensated with changes in the exposure time. Well, this is true, but the relationship is not always as direct as you might think. If the light level drops by half, doubling the exposure time will normally make up for it — but not if the exposure is already quite long. And the same thing happens at the other end of the scale. A doubling of the light level is not always catered for by halving the shutter speed.

The basic rule is that the exposure is equivalent to the light intensity (determined by the amount of light allowed through the lens, thus taking into account the aperture) multiplied by the exposure time. So we have a simple equation:

Exposure = Intensity × Time

Intensity and time are thus said to be reciprocal to one another. For any given exposure, an increase in one needs to be matched by a decrease in the other. With long exposures, however, the chemical processes taking place in the film emulsion are happening so slowly that the film may not be affected enough to form a sufficiently dense image, leading to under-exposure. With very brief exposures, it is all happening too fast for the emulsion to react, again giving under-exposure. In other words, the reciprocity between intensity and time has broken down.

As well as under-exposure, the problem also shows up as a colour cast. The three layers used in colour film — each sensitive to a different colour of light and dyed a different colour to make up the final image — react unequally, running into reciprocity problems at separate points. With long exposures, the result is normally a red or orange cast. With short exposures it is blue.

The point at which this takes place depends on the film. Emulsions designed for work under tungsten lighting, for example, assume you will be using comparatively long exposure times, and so are less prone to long-duration reciprocity law failure. Average daylight films run into the problem at around a second, and get progressively worse as the exposure times get longer. At the other end of the scale, you might get trouble when using 1/1000th, but you're more likely to have to go to 1/2000th before it shows up.

However, exposures using electronic flash can easily be as short as 1/20,000. The guide numbers and automatic exposure devices of flash guns are designed to take this into account and ensure a correct exposure level. But you are still likely to see some effects, in the form of a slight blue colour cast. Flash gun manufacturers often add a gold tint to the tube, reflector or lens of the unit to counter this, but if you have a problem it is easily corrected with an 81A amber filter, or an 05 yellow colour correction filter (some photographers tape gelatin versions of these over their flash units).

Correcting reciprocity law failure for long exposures is more difficult. Most film manufacturers publish figures for suggested exposure compensations. For example, if your meter suggests an exposure of 1 second, on Kodak Ektachrome 64, you should give it 1½ seconds (and a 15B blue colour correction filter). A good guide is to bracket exposures, giving the exposure time recommended by the meter plus other frames at 50 per cent, 100 per cent and — if the times are 10 seconds or more — 150 per cent of the suggested time.

OVERALL EXPOSURE

It may have occurred to you that photographing aircraft often puts conflicting demands on exposure settings. In particular, a fast moving subject can leave you wondering whether you should use a small stop, to get a large depth of field to cover up focusing errors, or open up for a fast shutter speed, to get rid of camera shake and subject blur.

The most truthful, but unhelpful, answer is that you need both. You need to make a decision at the time of shooting which is most important. You could probably work out a formula, taking into consideration the relative speed of the aircraft, the length of the lens, the amount of light and how many beers you had the night before. By the time you've done that, the pilot has finished the display and is already back in the bar. No, there is only one way to work it out — instinct. And the only way to develop that instinct is through practice. That said, here are a few starters.

Bright skies can easily knock back the exposure, resulting in an under-exposed subject

Begin by deciding on your *minima* — the largest aperture and longest shutter speed you can get away with. If you are shooting an aerial display, you might decide that ƒ5.6 and 1/125th will just about cover you in terms of depth of field and subject freezing. These are not the actual exposure settings — that comes next.

Let's say that you've set ƒ5.6. The meter tells you that a shutter speed of 1/1000th will give the correct exposure. This means you have three stops to play with. You could decide to shoot at 1/1000th, because the F-16 you're trying to photograph is moving fast, is jet-propelled (and so has no prop blades to freeze) and you are using a large and heavy 400 mm lens which is making your arms ache.

Alternatively, the subject might be a slow-moving power glider, coming close enough for you to use a compact 100 mm lens. However, the lens is not particularly fast, and you are worried about focusing errors. So you leave the shutter speed at 1/125th and use your extra three stops in closing the aperture down to ƒ16.

In practice, you'll find that the best solution is actually somewhere between the two. After all, with a fast F-16 you will be concerned about focusing accuracy too, and the best compromise may be to stop down to ƒ11 with a shutter speed of 1/250th, or maybe ƒ8 at 1/500th.

The final decision greatly depends on how good your (or your autofocus system's) focusing abilities are, and how good you are at holding the camera steady.

Conflict Diagram — Choosing the Shutter Speed

S	Freeze speed →	F
L	← *Blur props*	A
O	Camera shake →	S
W	← *Depth of field*	T

COMPENSATION

As we have already said, exposure meters can be fooled. The most common problem in aviation work is shooting aircraft in a bright sky. But other hazards include: bright reflections of the sun or lights in paintwork and canopies; dark subjects; light subjects.

Let's start with the most common problem. Unless an aeroplane is sufficiently large in the frame to determine the exposure, there is a danger that the metering system will take most of its information from the sky. 'This is a bright scene,' it decides, and knocks back the exposure a few stops. The result is a mid-grey sky and an aeroplane which is so under-exposed that it is nothing more than a featureless silhouette.

This can be a tricky problem to solve. Increasing the exposure might put some detail into the aircraft, although if the side you are looking at is in shadow this is by no means certain. And there is the danger that the sky will become over-exposed.

Finally, the problem does not always exist in the first place. If the aircraft is light-coloured, well lit and in a clear blue sky, you can most likely trust what your meter is telling you. So when do you take over, and by how much?

Lightly overcast, white skies are often the most dangerous. If the length of the aircraft fills less than half the width of the frame, you will probably want to increase exposure by a half to one stop. If the aircraft is dark-coloured, or somewhat in shadow, you may want to increase this to as much as a stop and a half. Whether you achieve this increase by opening up the lens to a larger aperture, or by selecting a slower shutter speed, is up to you, and depends on what settings you are starting with.

In very low light, you're likely to be using the lens at its maximum aperture. The shallow depth of field requires accurate focusing. Slight under-exposure can be used to create mood and allow a slightly faster shutter speed

Scenes which are generally light — a brightly-painted aircraft sitting on lig t-coloured concrete in broad daylight springs to mind — may also lead to under-exposure. Increasing exposure by
half to one stop helps here too.

If you are in fairly constant lighting conditions, such as a cloudless, sunny day, it's worth taking a few general meter readings to check against when you shoot. If you have a hand-held meter capable of doing incident readings, use that. Otherwise, aim the camera at the general landscape, with two-thirds of the frame filled with ground. Make sure there are no unusually light or dark subjects taking up a large proportion of your view. Then mentally note the suggested exposure. In times of doubt, you can always try shooting mid-way between this general setting and whatever your meter is suggesting at the time.

If you have any doubts about your exposure, and the shot is important, you can fall back on bracketing as a means of insurance. Bracketing means shooting several shots, varying the exposure with each one. Usually you will shoot at the settings you think are correct, plus two extra shots, one over-exposing and the other under-exposing by one stop. If you are *very* worried, you can shoot two more frames at two stops over and under.

Bracketing does use up film rather fast, but is better than missing the shot. Some of the more sophisticated, motordriven cameras now offer auto-bracketing, where a single press of the shutter button causes the camera to shoot three shots, with the exposure automatically varied. This can be handy in tricky, fast-moving situations, but should be turned off for normal conditions, where it is easier (and cheaper) simply to get the exposure right in the first place!

At the risk of losing some shadow detail, some people consistently under-expose colour transparency films by a third to a half stop — usually by changing the film speed setting — to increase colour saturation. This is purely a personal matter, but it's worth trying with your favourite film stock to see if you like the results.

Correcting the exposure on a manual camera is simply a matter of moving the relevant dial. But you can't do that with automatic cameras. At least one of the settings — aperture or shutter speed — is controlled by the camera. Altering the other setting will simply cause the camera to compensate, giving the same effective exposure that you started with.

Deliberate under-exposure by a stop or two can help hide irrelevant detail, but it needs a good, strong highlight to succeed

Fortunately, most automatic SLRs have some kind of device for deliberately modifying the exposure. The exposure override device is the most common. This is usually a dial, often directly linked to the film speed setting, which is used to force over- or under-exposure in third or half stops, up to a maximum of plus or minus two stops (sometimes three). You must remember to reset it to its neutral position when you are finished with it, and it's useful to have a camera which reminds you that the override is set with a sign in the viewfinder.

Using exposure override on an automatic camera is actually quite beneficial. It forces you to stop thinking strictly in terms of specific f- stops and shutter speeds and to start thinking in terms of exposure values. You quickly build up an instinct — you know, for example, that a certain type of backlighting or sky will need over-exposing by one stop.

A slightly faster way of working is to use an exposure lock, if fitted. This works by freezing the exposure setting when you press a button. You can then reframe the picture without the exposure being affected by any new areas of tone introduced into the shot.

If you have an aircraft sitting on the ramp, for example, you can set the exposure by pointing the camera at the general landscape, hold down the exposure lock button, and then swing round to aim at the aircraft. Exposure lock is most useful with metering systems that are quite heavily centre-weighted or have spot-metering facilities. You can then aim the centre of the frame at an area of the subject which you want to come out as mid-grey in the picture, lock the exposure and then compose. This is a variation of a technique known as 'key tone' metering.

If you are using a motordrive, check whether your exposure stays locked while you hold the button down, even after you've fired the first frame. Some revert to normal metering again, and you have to release the exposure lock button and repeat the process.

If your camera has no exposure override or lock, you can achieve the same effect using the film speed setting. By fooling the system into thinking that you have suddenly switched to a different speed of film you can get it to change the exposure. For example, if you have ISO 100 film loaded, turning the film speed dial to ISO 50 will result in over-exposure by one stop. However, if you do use this method, get into the habit of turning the dial back to the correct setting immediately after taking your shot. There is nothing worse than discovering you have shot an entire roll of fantastic pictures all at the wrong film speed setting!

Some modern cameras, including most of the new generation of compact models, read the film speed directly from the cassette using a system known as DX coding. Coded films have a black and silver checkerboard design printed on them. The camera has pins which connect with the pattern and read the pattern electrically (the silver squares conduct electricity, the black ones don't). If your camera uses this system, then you don't have the option of fiddling with the film speed setting.

FILTERING

There are two types of filtering — compensation and effect. Compensation filtering means returning the picture to something that looks normal. Without the filter, the picture would have an unnatural-looking colour cast. Filtering for effect means introducing an extra element into the picture to jazz it up a little — a deliberate colour cast, perhaps, or a 'starburst' effect on highlights.

An 81A amber filter has been used here to emphasise the moody colours of the sunset

CORRECTION

When your eye is subject to a strong colour cast, a combination of retinal fatigue and compensation by the brain corrects the colours, attempting to return the scene to some kind of normal colour balance. Film is not so adaptable. This is why some scenes that appear quite normal — such as artificially-lit rooms — need filtering.

The most common situation which requires correction filtering is in rooms bathed in artificial light. Tungsten lights, including domestic bulbs, give a strong amber cast on ordinary film. Fluorescent lights are even worse, giving off a sickly green light.

There is one way of getting around the amber cast without using filters, and that is by using tungsten balanced film. Normal colour film is designed to give accurate colour so long as the light source itself is of a standard colour — known as 'photographic daylight'. To help standardize this colour, photographic scientists developed a system for measuring colour, calibrated in degrees Kelvin. This is normally a measurement of temperature (similar to Celsius but starting at absolute zero rather than the freezing point of water) and the system is known as 'colour temperature'. The definition of colour temperature involves a theoretical black body. When heated, this body gives off light, the colour of which depends on the temperature. It's rather like a poker in a fire — it starts black, turns red as it gets hot, and then white as it gets hotter still.

Standard daylight is said to have a colour temperature of 5,500K. Photographic light bulbs, which are redder, have a lower colour temperature — around 3,400K. As some photographers like to work with tungsten lighting, it is possible to get film which is balanced to 3,400K, rather than 5,500K. This 'tungsten' film gives normal colours when photographic lamps are used, although domestic light bulbs, which have a colour temperature of under 3,000K, would still give a slight amber cast.

But using tungsten film can be a pain. It means you have to carry around two types of film — if you used tungsten film in daylight you would get a strong blue cast. Tungsten film is not as readily available as daylight types. And quite often you want to take just a few shots under tungsten lighting, not a whole roll.

So for the aviation photographer, faced with shooting the occasional picture in a hangar or museum, filtering is a much better solution to colour problems than special films.

Correcting colour can be a tricky business. Still life and fashion photographers, concerned with getting 100 per cent accurate colour, will spend hours trying fine variations in filtration, using pale and subtle gelatin filters to make tiny corrections.

Fortunately, the aviation photographer is less worried about 100 per cent accuracy. So long as the colour cast is not intrusive, then a slight imbalance rarely matters. So the corrections for artificial lighting can be achieved with a couple of filters.

The Kodak system of Wratten numbers has been most widely adopted for describing filters. The 80-series filters — 80A, B and C in ascending order of density — are deep blue in colour and are designed for shooting tungsten-lit scenes with daylight film. The 80A is the best all-rounder. Should you not want to get rid of the cast completely, but just knock it back a little, the paler 82-series filters are useful.

With fluorescent lighting, which you are likely to encounter in museums and hangars, you have less of a choice in that filtration is the only answer — there are no fluorescent-balanced films. The answer here is a magenta filter, and the most useful is usually called a '30M' — the 30 refers to the number of colour correction units. These can often be bought specifically as 'fluorescent-day', 'FL-D' or 'F-D' filters.

You have to be careful with fluorescent lighting, however. The colour various enormously depending on the type of light tube in use. Some are even designed to give out something approaching 'daylight' colour (in practice usually around 4,800K). When you work under fluorescent lights always take two shots of everything — with and without the filter.

You may occasionally need correction filters outdoors, too.

A polarizing filter has slightly darkened the sky. It's best to use these filters with some restraint otherwise the effect is predictable and overpowering

Without doubt, the most useful filter for the aviation photographer is the 81A. This is a pale amber filter, sometimes referred to as a 'warm' filter. That's because it makes the picture look a little warmer, without inducing any radical colour shifts.

It is difficult to lay down hard and fast rules about when to use a warm filter, but there are guide-lines. For example, when there is a heavy overcast — one of those dreary, dull days — the light tends to be quite blue. You might not notice it, but it does show up on photographs. That's precisely when you need an 81A. And it can prove useful on misty or hazy days. It is also useful when there is snow on the ground, which reflects a lot of ultra-violet, also giving a blue cast.

Indeed, there are photographers who leave 81A filters on their lenses for everything but bright, sunny days.

It can also improve results on days with cloudless, blue skies. Anything falling in shadow — and that could easily include the sides or parts of aeroplanes — is lit by the blue sky, rather than the sun. You will need the warm filter to get rid of the resulting blue cast. And flash pictures benefit from some warming too. The very short exposure that flash gives the film leads to the previously mentioned problem of reciprocity law failure. The most noticeable effect of this is a colour cast — in the case of short exposures it is normally a slightly blue cast, which can make the shot look cold and washed-out. An 81A solves this although, if your flash system is not one of the latest types using through-the-lens metering, you will need to open up the aperture slightly to compensate for the filter's ⅓ of a stop loss of light.

Photographers sometimes use the light blue 82 filter for partially correcting the red glow near sunrise and sunset. However, most people like that light precisely for that red colour — it's up to you.

Your problems really start when there is a mixture of lighting. In a museum, you are quite likely to have a mixture of fluorescent and tungsten artificial lighting, with perhaps a bit of daylight coming in through windows and skylights. Your job is to try to assess which is the dominant lighting: if they are all fairly equal the best solution is not to filter at all.

It is a mistake to try to judge the effect of a filter simply by holding it up to the light, or even putting it on the front of the lens and looking through the camera. Filters have a much greater effect on film than they do on the eye, because of the brain's ability to correct colour bias. Remember this when trying to assess the effect of a particular filter on the picture you are about to take. If in doubt, use a lighter filter, or none at all.

POLARIZING
There is a kind of knee-jerk reaction among some photographers who, when they see a beautiful, clear blue sky, feel compelled to slap a polarizing filter on their lens. And it's true that the effect can be dramatic. By cutting out 'scattered' light, polarizing filters can make the colours in your pictures much more intense. Skies take on a beautiful, deep colour, with pure white clouds.

The way polarizing filters work is really quite clever. Imagine you are looking head-on at a beam of light, and are able to see the vibration of the light waves. This wave forms a plane, running along the light beam. But there are many of these planes at all angles to the centre point. The polarizing filter acts like a grille, or set of bars. If the plane of vibration is in the same direction as the gaps between the bars, that bit of light will pass through. All the other light waves, whose planes of vibration are at angles to the grille, will be stopped.

One result is that the amount of light getting through is reduced, and a polarizing filter will cost you two or three stops. However, the light that does get through is in a more coherent form: a lot of the scattered light is cut out. The effect is greatest on light which is already partially polarized. Air particles have the effect of polarizing sunlight. If the polarizing filter is set so that its plane of polarization is at an angle to the light from the sky, the amount of light is reduced and so the sky looks darker. That's why polarizing filters are made so that they can be rotated once on your lens — so you can make the most of these effects.

One slight problem you may come across is that some camera light meters are confused by this single-plane light, and may give under-exposed pictures. The solution is to use a circular polarizer, which uses an extra layer (known as a quarter wave retardation plate, for those who like jargon) to give the polarized light a twist, so that it forms a helix, rather than a flat plane. All meter systems are happy with this type of light. Alas, not all camera manuals tell you that you need this kind of filter, so if in doubt, buy circular polarizers.

The polarizer can be used to increase contrast and make colours look more saturated. The effect varies depending on the direction of the light, being most pronounced when the sun is at right angles to your line of sight.

The other benefit of a polarizer is in killing reflections. Because scattered light is excluded, the filter can help to cut through the glare on a cockpit canopy or remove unwanted reflections from glossy paint schemes. This largely applies to static aircraft: as you have to revolve the filter to get the best result, it is difficult to do with the split-second timing needed for moving objects.

UV

Although most photographers have UV (ultra-violet) filters, few use them for actually filtering out unwanted light. And there are good reasons for that. The fact is that the glass used in many modern lenses filters out almost as much UV light as these filters. And what remains has precious little effect on the film.

When it does show up, excess ultra-violet gives a blue cast to the picture. The place where you are most likely to see it is in snow-bound scenes, where the light from clear skies is reflected in the snow. Even then, most of the blue cast is caused by the colour of the sky.

So why buy a UV filter? The answer is that it is cheaper than the lens. When prop wash or slipstream throws a piece of grit at your camera, which would you rather have it hit — an inexpensive filter or the front element of a lens costing ten or twenty times as much?

Aviation photographers spend a lot of time working in breezes of one kind or another, usually artificially created. This is especially true of those brave souls who are prone to strapping cameras to wings or hanging out of the side of aircraft. Dust and other flying debris is a constant hazard, and a UV filter will not just protect your lens, it will make cleaning easier. If the filter clogs up with dust and you need to shoot straight away, just take the filter off, or replace it with another, until you've got time to get around to cleaning it. It's worth having at least one UV filter for each of your lenses, plus a couple of spares for just such contingencies.

If you want to use another filter — a polarizer or 81A perhaps — the UV filter should be removed first. Every extra glass surface you introduce in front of the lens is another dust trap which can lead to some degradation of the image quality. And if the filters are less than optically perfect (as is often the case) using more than one compounds the problem. What's more, having several filters stuck on the front of the lens can lead to vignetting where the filter mount cuts off the edges of the picture.

Incidentally, when shops are out of stock of UV filters, they will often try to sell you 1B skylight filters instead, claiming that they are the same thing. They are not. Skylight filters have a slight pink tint, giving a slight warming effect to the picture, though not as effective as an 81A. Although, as we have seen, pictures often need some warming-up, you don't want it all the time. So don't be palmed off with excuses. If you want a filter to leave on at all times, for protection, get a UV.

FILTERING FOR EFFECT
When using filters for effect, always ask yourself what the filter is adding to the picture, and whether it is really appropriate. The answers are often 'Nothing' and 'No' respectively.

GRADUATED FILTERS
The main exception to the rule is the graduated filter, in which the colour occupies only half the filter area, and the border between the tinted and plain areas is 'smudged'. Indeed, graduated filters don't really deserve to be included in the special effects category. When they are used with discretion you often don't notice their presence. However, most people lump them with the likes of diffraction and starburst filters because grads first became generally popular with the advent of filter systems.

Cinematographers have used grads for years. For one thing, they are useful for darkening bright skies. If you expose for the ground, or an object on it, the sky may 'burn out' becoming a featureless white expanse. This is especially true of lightly overcast skies. By knocking back the light from the sky by a stop or two, the grad filter helps retain any detail there might be, and stops the sky from dominating the shot.

Neutral grey grads are made for that purpose, but the most popular versions of this type of filter are the coloured grads. They can be used to add a bit of colour to a grey scene. However, you should be wary of using grads to put drama into pictures. Everything might look wonderful through the viewfinder, but a whole roll of pictures with bright orange skies becomes extremely tedious. Still, there's nothing wrong with occasional use, especially if you use a suitable colour.

Grads usually come in two strengths, and bearing in mind the fact that the effect is always greater on film than on the eye, the lighter shades are usually much more useful. And avoid stopping down the lens too much. Although the filter is so close to the lens that it is unlikely to show up sharply, smaller stops do bring the borderline between tinted and plain regions slightly more into focus, making the transition in the picture more abrupt. The same is true of using wide angle lenses. A shot using a grad used on a 24 mm lens at $f16$ will look artificial. Try to stick to $f5.6$ or $f8$, opening up a bit if you switch to very wide angle lenses — 24 mm or wider.

SPECIAL EFFECTS

The term 'special effects filter' covers a host of sins. It could mean a soft focus filter which turns your expensive lens into something with the optical characteristics of a milk bottle. It might be a prism which tries to turn a dull scene into an interesting one by including it several times in the frame. Or it might introduce all kinds of fuzzy distortions into the picture, such as the starburst filters which turn points of light into radiating spokes, or the refraction filter which turns the same points into umbrellas of rainbow light.

There are times when it is tempting to think that special effects filters should be banned, or one should need a licence to use them. At the very least, they should carry government health warnings. Like guns, it is not the filters themselves that are dangerous, but the people who use them. And like guns, they are all too often the tools of desperate people.

This is a matter of personal taste, but it is highly improbable that a picture can be saved by using a special effects filter. However, it is easy to ruin one that way.

Sticking a soft focus filter in front of the lens does not instantly make the picture more romantic, nor does a starburst or diffraction filter automatically add impact or excitement. The truth is, these kind of special effects are dreadfully predictable and hackneyed, unless used with extreme care and (this is the almost impossible bit) subtlety. Even worse, the effects often detract from the real impact of the picture — the aircraft itself.

EXPOSURE CORRECTIONS

Sticking a piece of coloured glass in front of the lens does have one unfortunate effect — it cuts down the amount of light getting into the camera. This is not a problem with clear, special effects or UV filters, but with anything tinted it has to be taken into account.

If you are using through-the-lens metering — as is most likely — then the light reducing effect of the filter is automatically taken into account. Otherwise you need to apply a filter factor when calculating exposure. The filter factor number is supplied with the filter. If the factor is 2, it means that only half the light is getting through and you need to give an extra stop of exposure — either open up the lens one stop, or give a slower shutter speed. A factor of 4 means two stops, 8 means three and so on.

Even if you are using TTL metering, you have to be careful. A grad filter, for example, makes life a little complicated for the metering system. It is best to do your metering first, which will then give a correct exposure for the part of the image covered by the clear half of the filter, and then fit the filter. If in doubt, bracket your exposures.

AIR-TO-AIR

If you should get close enough to another aircraft to take decent pictures while on a scheduled airline flight, then you should contact the nearest national newspaper as soon as you land — you will almost certainly make the front page with a 'near miss' story!

Occasionally you will be treated to a photo opportunity, such as doing a formation landing with another airliner at an airport with parallel runways. On the whole, however, if you want to take pictures of a flying aircraft from another aircraft, you will have to set it up yourself.

Some of the most exciting air-to-air shots you see in books and magazines have been taken by military aircrews, as they are among the few who get the opportunity for this sort of thing supplied on a plate. The rest of us have to work at setting up an air-to-air shoot, but it can be done, even if you don't necessarily wind up with pictures of the latest fighters.

The basic problem, of course, is that you need at least two aircraft in the air at the right time. The easiest solution to this problem is to throw money at it. However, hiring two aircraft, with pilots, for an hour — which is the minimum time you're likely to get away with if you want to stand a reasonable chance of getting a range of good shots — can be a financially depressing experience. You will also need to find a sympathetic operation which will agree to scrub the sortie without charge should the weather be not quite to your liking — a dull, overcast day may be good enough to fly in, but the light won't exactly make your pictures sing, and if you did fly you might end up wasting your money. On the other hand, you might need a day with a slight haze, as it's often useful for masking an unattractive background and highlighting the aircraft.

If you are a pilot and have access to an aircraft, the hassle and the cost are greatly reduced: now you need only one other aircraft and pilot. But be careful: it *is* possible to fly and shoot at the same time — military pilots frequently do it — and you *can* always use the autopilot to hold your aircraft straight and level while the other formates on it. But either approach hampers your creativity and can be dangerous. You are well advised to concentrate on one job at a time, which means leaving the flying to someone else.

The situation is much easier if you find someone who wants pictures taken of their pet aeroplane and is prepared to at least split the costs, or perhaps even pick up the entire tab for the flying. Failing that, it's a matter of having friends with aeroplanes or taking the pictures on assignment, where someone else pays the bill. If you do get to go up you will want to make the most of your air time, so let's have a look at some of the techniques and pitfalls.

GENERAL

The first thing you should do is have a decent breakfast. Swanning around the skies with a part-full stomach can lead to embarrassing moments when you hit turbulence. If you are in the slightest doubt about your stomach's abilities to hold on to meals, swallow some travel sickness pills and take an emergency sick-bag. Few pilots will see this as an admission of weakness but will, instead, admire your forethought and willingness to keep their aircraft clean! If you are about to ride in the back seat of a fast jet, these precautions become mandatory.

Wear the right clothes. Even in summer an open or unheated cockpit can get cold once you start putting some distance between you and the ground. The temperature drops by 2°C for every thousand feet of altitude, and the slipstream may cool you down even more. Again, take the advice of the pilot.

Check with the pilot about where you can stash equipment and camera bags. If possible, carry everything you need in your

own pockets, although make sure the gear will be easily accessible once you are seated and strapped in. You really won't need much in the way of kit. With film, however, try to estimate how much you will use — then double it. There's no popping back to pick up a few rolls when you run out. Leave the film boxes at home — they take up a lot of space — but keep the film in the plastic canisters for safety.

Make sure all your gear is secure, with loose items stashed safely in buttoned or zipped pockets. Should the pilot put on any negative-*g* your stuff could end up flying around the cockpit. Apart from being generally uncomfortable, and the danger of knocking the pilot unconscious with a camera or lens, something could get stuck under the controls. Either way, you'll be very unpopular.

Above (left): Shooting out of a dirty window — in this case the door window of a KC-130F tanker — can soften the picture and lower contrast.
(Right): Use the lens reasonably close to a clean window and you might not even know it's there

If you are using an open doorway or window, you might like to rig your gear with safety lines where possible. Thin nylon cord attached to you or some convenient bit of the airframe should do the job. And watch out when changing film. The slipstream can be nasty and so can flying flotsam (it might be wise to clean the cockpit before flight).

Once you are safely tied down to your seat, you can start thinking about the photography. The rules are pretty much the same as for ground-based photography, although some have a special relevance in air-to-air work. For example, you need to watch the edges of the frame — struts, propellers, wheels and wings have a nasty habit of sneaking into the picture. If you can't get rid of them, use them as a compositional detail.

It can be tricky to keep the camera still in an aircraft which is buzzing with engine vibration and bucking around in turbulence. However, don't try to steady the camera by resting it or the hand holding it against the fuselage or window frame. Aircraft vibration will be transmitted straight to the camera making the problem even worse. The solution is to use a suitably fast shutter speed — 1/250th or faster is a good idea if the subject allows. Mind you, if you're photographing a propeller driven aircraft, you won't want to go much faster because of the risk of freezing the prop. If you must rack the speed down to 1/125th or 1/60th you should pay extra attention to keeping the camera steady, and this is largely a matter of practice. If in any doubt about how still you're keeping the camera, take several shots at different speeds. It's a lot cheaper to use extra film than to pay for another sortie because the first shots didn't work.

Vibration and camera shake are always exaggerated by long lenses. Using a 300 mm in flight is really pushing your luck. It's probably best to regard 100 mm as the longest practical lens, and use shorter lengths if you can.

CLEAR VIEW

Ideally, you need a clear view out of the aircraft, unobstructed by glass or Perspex. Windows and canopies are rarely in perfect condition. At the very least, they tend to be thick. At worst, they will be scratched, dirty and cloudy after long exposure to the sun. Bringing along some window cleaner and having a good scrub before take-off will undoubtedly help — although make sure you get permission first! Even so, the glass or Perspex is unlikely to be as clear as you'd like.

Only a few, rare aeroplanes are fitted with optically flat glass. Even the direct vision panels in aeroplanes, designed to give the pilot an undistorted view, are far from perfect for taking pictures: photographers and pilots have different criteria for judging optical perfection!

The best option is to remove something. Sometimes windows can be opened, even in ways they are not meant to be. For example, by removing a couple of screws from the window stays, the windows on a Cessna 172 will open right out. Once they are horizontal, the air flow across the wings holds them in place. However, they do need to be opened slowly, with a firm grip. Letting go too soon causes them to fly up, possibly hitting the wing and perhaps parting company with the aircraft. And in addition to getting the owner's permission to do this in the first place, you should warn the pilot each time before opening the window. He or she may want to slow down to avoid potential damage to the aircraft.

On other small aircraft, windows or doors can be removed completely, although this calls for skill on the part of the pilot in coping with the asymmetrically disturbed airflow, and you need both nerve and complete faith in your seat belt.

You have to be a little careful about sticking your camera out too far. Remember that, even in a light aircraft, you will be doing something in excess of 90 knots — often much more. The

Few people get the opportunity for air-to-air photography. But shooting at a point along the runway just after take-off, preferably from a high vantage point, and getting the aircraft just after wheels-up, looks a lot like air-to-air

next time you're driving at 50 mph down a road, try sticking your hand out of the window. You'll feel quite a force on it, trying to blow it back. Now imagine twice as much force on a hand which is clutching a camera costing a month's salary. It's enough to make you very twitchy.

The situation is even worse in a helicopter where the slipstream is joined by a downdraught sufficient to keep several tons of metal in the air. At the very least it will induce severe camera shake. At worst, you could lose the camera. That's not to say you shouldn't attempt it. Dramatic pictures can be taken by holding the camera outside a window and shooting your own aircraft, using a wide angle lens. But be prepared

for a stiff breeze, and use a fast shutter speed — 1/500th or faster.

If you must shoot through windows — and fighter pilots are loath to remove the canopies of their aircraft — watch out for internal reflections. Wear dark clothing including a pair of thin black gloves. Any light objects will show up as out-of-focus reflections and can ruin an otherwise perfect shot.

If you find yourself suffering a great deal from internal reflections off the canopy, you can use the rubber hood trick. A rubber lens shade on the front of the lens can be pushed up against the glass. This cuts out reflections while also avoiding transmitting aircraft vibration as a metal lens hood would do (one of the few times a rubber hood is better than the metal variety). To get away with this, you need a nice clean patch on the canopy, without scratches or distortions. Using a wide angle lens helps a little, as it uses more of the glass and so any imperfections assume less importance.

This is an important general point: you will also find that shooting through glass limits the type of lens you can use. If you use a long focal length lens, the narrow angle of view means you are looking through a small section of the window. Any small imperfections take up a large part of the image, leading to diffusion of the light — a soft focus effect — and shape distortions. A wide angle lens, on the other hand, uses a large proportion of the window, and the faults are smaller and less significant.

Your subject aircraft should be moving in the same direction and pretty much at the same speed as the machine you are sitting in. This means that its speed relative to you is very small, so focusing should not present much of a problem. It also means you don't need much in the way of depth of field, to cover focusing errors, which is good news: every extra bit of depth brings the canopy and all its imperfections more into focus, which is less than desirable. Go for a wide stop — around $f4$ or $f5.6$. This will keep the glass blurred and give you a fast shutter speed.

Getting close to the window also helps, but get too close and you have a similar problem to that posed by telephotos — shooting through a small section of the glass. With 35 mm or 50 mm lenses, get back about six inches from the glass, and go slightly closer with wider lenses (they have more depth of field).

When possible, shoot with the camera square-on to the window, rather than at an angle to it. By looking through the window at an angle you are effectively increasing the amount of glass in the way.

Shooting into the sun emphasises the imperfections too, showing up every little scratch and mark. If this becomes too much of a problem, get the sun behind you, or at least to one side. In any case, your subject will be better lit this way, unless you are going for a silhouette, or mood shot.

Even if the sortie is not primarily for your benefit — as is generally the case on military hops — don't be afraid to ask the pilots to move the aircraft around. In the case of shots which include the ground, a steep angle of bank can add quite considerably to the picture's appeal.

WORKING WITH PILOTS

Getting the sun and the aeroplanes in the right place requires good co-ordination with the pilots. Indeed, the success of any sortie depends as much on the pilots as on your own photographic skills.

For a start, make sure you get the right kind of pilots. You need both fliers to be experienced in formation work. The average weekend pilot will start to get nervous if the aircraft are closer than a few hundred feet. Even if you find pilots capable of holding station on each other, they are likely to waste your valuable time getting into the same bit of airspace. Formation flying is a skill, and one that not all pilots are blessed with. If you can find only one pilot with this skill, put him or her in the target aircraft. While the pilot of your camera ship flies straight and level, the target aircraft pilot can formate on you.

It's important to give the pilots a full briefing before you get into the aeroplane. If you're going up with just the one aircraft, things are a little simpler as you can discuss changes to the plan with the pilot. Even so, flight plans need to be filed beforehand, and last minute changes in the air can cause all sorts of problems.

In an air-to-air sortie, all pilots need to know what is going on. Sudden changes in plan and poor communications in the air can be more than inconvenient — they can be positively fatal. And there is a limit to how effectively you can work if everything has to be relayed over the radio, to which you are unlikely to have direct access anyway. If you can use the radio, do so. But make sure you have a firm grasp of the technology. A quick R/T course at a local flying school might help. Keep everyone constantly updated.

It's helpful to work out a series of unambiguous hand signals, to get the pilot of the subject aircraft to move relative to your own. Make sure everyone understands what they mean before you leave the ground. And once you're in the air, make sure your signals can be seen. If you are directly between the sun and the subject aircraft, don't be surprised if the pilot of that aeroplane — who is now seeing you in silhouette while squinting into the glare of the sun — misses your signals.

Always take the pilot's advice, even if you think you're not getting what you need. That doesn't mean you shouldn't ask for something, unless you know it to be unnecessary or dangerous. For example, you might want the target aircraft to fly knife-edge to get a shot of the top or bottom, or perhaps inverted for something a little unusual. But if a pilot is reticent about doing something it is probably for a good reason — it might be beyond the pilot's abilities, or there could be technical objections. But don't ask them to do anything silly — they might do it! Pilots are only human and have egos like anyone else, only more so.

Naturally, the aircraft have to be well matched. Trying to shoot a fast jet from a Cessna is unlikely to be too successful. Sure, you can get a passing shot, but then you have to waste time and fuel waiting for the subject to come round again. Even if the subject can slow down enough, it's likely to have flaps and even undercarriage hanging in the breeze, which could spoil your shot. Both aircraft need to be able to cruise at the same speed — and preferably with something in reserve. If you get out of position, it's nice to have some extra speed to cut down the amount of time you spend trying to formate.

Finally, make sure you have full clearance for anything you want to do, especially if it's something out of the ordinary and involves the air space around the airfield. This should be the pilot's responsibility, but it doesn't hurt to double-check.

REMOTE CONTROL

There are many situations in which your camera can get stunning shots, but where it would be unwise for you to accompany it. Standing by the side of the runway to get aircraft rotating or landing is fine — providing you have permission — but shooting from the end of the runway, or very close to the edge can be hazardous for both you and the occupants of the aeroplane.

Hanging on to the outside of an aeroplane is even more detrimental to your health. Yet strapping a camera on a wing strut, the wing itself, the top of the tail and so on, is an excellent way of getting spectacular shots of your aeroplane. Professional aviation photographers also use rear-facing cameras strapped to an aircraft's tail for air-to-air shots of other aeroplanes.

Even when you are close to the camera, it may not be possible to operate it directly. If you want pictures of the pilot, for example, a camera strapped to the front of the cockpit is one way to get it, and can be especially effective with open-cockpit biplanes.

All these cases share one problem — you can't be there to trip the shutter. Fortunately, there are several ways of doing this remotely.

EQUIPMENT

Unless you fancy going outside to wind-on the film, a motordrive is essential for remote photography. There may be situations in which you want to shoot sequences, but most of the time you need just a single-frame capability, and so even an inexpensive autowind will do the job. The main requirement is that the drive can be easily triggered.

The simplest method of firing the camera remotely is to stick it on a tripod, start the self-timer and run away. This ludicrous approach is, of course, hopelessly hit-and-miss and of little value. It is only mentioned to highlight the fact that you do need to retain some control even when you are not actually holding the camera.

One step up is to use a cable release. These simple devices screw into the shutter release button and a plunger at one end pushes out a rod at the other to trip the shutter. Cable releases are normally used where you want to avoid vibrating the camera, as tends to happen when you push the button directly. As such, they are rarely over a couple of feet long. That may be enough for a camera mounted inside a cockpit, but is hopeless if you want to put the camera outside. Even if you could get a cable release sufficiently long, its elasticity over that length would make it unreliable.

A development of the cable release, designed specifically for greater distances, is the pneumatic release. Squeezing a plastic bulb causes increased pressure in a long, thin tube, about the thickness of electrical cable, which activates a plunger at the remote end, screwed into the cable release socket. The length of the tube can be anything up to ten metres. Once again, however, reliability is a little dubious. Over-vigorous squeezing of the bulb can result in the tube becoming detached at some point. And the tube is unlikely to stand up to the rigours of being taped to the outside of an aircraft.

As we have already seen, the remote camera will almost certainly

A remotely mounted camera mounted in an open window or outside aircraft can get shots you might find difficult otherwise. A 15 mm lens has been used here to ensure the maximum subject coverage

have a motordrive attached, and we can use this to provide a more reliable way of firing the camera. As they use electrical shutter releases, rather than mechanical, most motordrives can be fired using a plain electrical switch. Somewhere on the drive you should find a socket. This may take a standard jack plug or might require a special plug, but either way the wires coming from the plug will be just two ordinary single-strand cables. When connected to make a circuit, they fire the camera and operate the motordrive.

Camera manufacturers make their own remote control triggers, but they are rarely more than simple switches, and you can probably make up your own. Nikon, for example, sell a piece of wire with the correct motordrive plug at one end and two banana-type plugs at the other, making it easy to construct your own switch. However, you should always check with the manufacturer first, before making up your own cables, in case you void any warranties.

Electrical cables are far more robust than cable releases or pneumatic tubes, and this type of arrangement is more than adequate for a wide variety of situations. However, there is one big drawback to all three methods, and that's the necessity to run cables between you and the camera. Aircraft owners may object to you drilling holes in the airframe to accommodate the wires, and setting up the link can take a lot of time. And wires on the outside of the aircraft can be a hazard if they get loose.

A wireless link avoids these problems, and two types are available: infra-red and radio. Infra-red systems work on a similar principle to a TV or video remote control. A coded pulse of infra-red 'light' from a hand unit is recognised by a receiver, in this case attached to the camera. Simple devices will fire the shutter and cycle the motordrive once for each press of the hand unit's button. More sophisticated units allow continuous firing with the motordrive, and are capable of operating two or more cameras by using different codes for each receiver.

Infra-red does have some serious limitations for this kind of application. One problem is that of ambient light. The signal from the trigger may be so weak compared with daylight, navigation and landing lights and so on, that it may be lost completely. Even if it works on the ground, there is no guarantee it will work in the air, when you might have increased reflectance from clouds or water. The effectiveness is further lowered when you are aiming the hand unit through cockpit glass, which reflects part of the signal. Even worse, it is possible for the receiver to be triggered by stray light, wasting your

Below (left): Strong side lighting, such as that from a setting sun, shows up texture and surface detail. (Right): A low winter sun gives a strong light providing contrast which can be used to add drama to otherwise ordinary shots

valuable film and leaving you in the position of thinking you have more frames left than there really are.

The other drawback with infra-red is that, for all practical purposes, it is line-of-sight only. Nothing must come between the transmitter and receiver, which severely limits the places where you can put the receiver. Of course, the camera and receiver do not necessarily have to be in the same place, but by the time you start running cables between them, you might as well use an ordinary electric release, which is more reliable anyway.

Radio systems do not suffer from this problem. The transmitter and receiver don't even have to be on the same aircraft. Most of the professional camera manufacturers produce radio triggering systems, and it is also possible to concoct your own using commercially available hand-held radios or model aeroplane systems. If you do go for the DIY approach, however, check with the relevant authorities about any necessary licences and restricted frequencies.

Aircraft are subject to a lot of radio 'noise', including interference from the engine and signals from the radio and navigational instruments. It's a good idea to run a full set of tests with the aeroplane you intend to use before getting airborne, otherwise your film could be used up without you knowing it.

The range of lenses you can use is quite limited. If you are trying to get pictures of the camera aircraft itself, perhaps from a camera strapped to a strut or wing, you will need a wide angle lens to get enough of it in shot — possibly as wide as a 24 mm, or even 20 mm. The same is true for in-cockpit shots. Telephotos are far too prone to vibration, and have too narrow a field of view to be useful for this kind of work.

Watch our for your own shadow when the sun is low

Even for air-to-air shots you will need a wide lens. As you will almost certainly be shooting blind, you need a wide field of view to increase your chances of getting the subject aircraft in shot, and the vibration problem still applies. Again, a 24 mm or 20 mm lens is a good choice, although you might be able to do something useful with a 35 mm. If the pilots you are using are good, getting the subject aircraft up close to the camera with a 20 mm lens fitted can give sensational results.

The most important characteristic of any piece of equipment used for remote photography, from the camera to the triggering device, is that it is completely reliable. You can't easily get to the equipment to unjam something. And if the gear is being used on the outside of an aircraft it will be subjected to high winds and low temperatures. One small malfunction can completely ruin a shoot, which can turn out to be an expensive problem if you are paying for flying time.

Low temperature is a special hazard, and one which is all too often ignored. When you're high, with the camera gear hanging in the breeze, all sorts of things can happen. If you're really unlucky you might get icing. The batteries might fail or the shutter jam. Short of taping a hot water bottle to the camera, there's little you can do. The main precaution is to protect the gear from the slipstream, particularly the battery compartments.

TECHNIQUE

Some of the potential pitfalls can be avoided by making sure the camera is properly mounted. For shots on the ground, this is easy. A tripod is all you need, although if you want a really low angle, one of those mini-tripods is useful — Leitz and Minolta make excellent examples. If you can't find a suitable spot to set up a tripod, you could try using one of those special G-clamps which come fitted with a ball and socket head.

When it comes to fitting the camera to an aircraft, on the other hand, a G-clamp is hardly likely to be enough. Although it may be robust enough to mount inside a cockpit, out in the rough environment of the slipstream you need something far tougher. You will probably have to build some kind of special mount, as few aircraft come fitted with ball and socket heads as part of the standard equipment. And the type of mount will vary depending on where you want to put the camera, and on the type of aircraft.

Basically, the mount should screw into the tripod socket of the camera, but it is useful to have some straps holding the camera tightly, or the pressures on the tripod mount could cause internal damage to the camera.

Some stiff rubber will cut out some of the vibration, although if there is too much padding the shaking might get worse. If you make up some kind of clamp — to go on a wing strut, perhaps — use wood and/or rubber for the surfaces of the clamps. This will avoid scratching or denting the paintwork.

Make sure that any screws are tight. Airframes suffer a great deal of vibration during flight, and it is all too easy for screws to work loose. It is a disheartening sight to watch your expensive camera and motordrive spontaneously detach themselves from the aircraft — not to mention the likelihood of crippling law suits should they hit anyone on the way down. As a safety measure, you can drill small holes through any fixing bolts, just behind the in-flight positions of the tightening nuts, and insert split rings, to stop the nuts, and the camera, coming off completely.

Be liberal with the gaffer tape. Aircraft slipstreams are vicious and will find every little nook and cranny of the equipment. Generously covering the equipment in gaffer tape will not only help it to stay in one piece, it will also seal it. In particular, tape the camera back shut and seal up the edges, and tape the lens focusing and aperture rings once you have focused and set the camera for the right exposure.

The harsh midday light is not so bad if the aircraft is brightly coloured. Indeed, it helps to make the most of the colour, although you have to be careful how you treat shadows

Exposure can be tricky. Automatic exposure is useful if there is likely to be any change in the light — it's difficult to go out there to open up the lens while you're in flight. However, auto-exposure systems can be fooled by occasional highlights, so if it is a cloudless, sunny day you might like to set it on manual. Don't be tempted to use auto-bracketing systems; by rattling off three frames every time you hit the button they eat film very rapidly.

If you do use automatic — which is most likely — you will need to block out the viewfinder. Without your head to get in the way, a significant amount of light can enter the viewfinder with the danger that it will confuse the metering system. Some cameras, such as the Nikon F3 High Eyepoint finder, are fitted with viewfinder shutters for precisely this reason. Flipping a switch (which should be gaffer-taped in position) blocks out the

Below: Overcast conditions give a softer light with better shadow detail (left) than direct sunlight (right).

finder. If you don't have this feature, gaffer tape across the finder itself should do the trick.

You should aim for a nice fast shutter speed, to reduce the effects of vibration. A speed of 1/500th should do the job, although if you can get faster, do. Loading fast film — ISO 200 if you're shooting slides, and perhaps ISO 400 if you're using negative film — will help, but only if you don't mind the extra grain and slight loss of sharpness. If you are shooting transparencies and normally use ISO 50 or 64 film, you might like to consider going up to ISO 100. Even one stop of extra speed is worth it.

If you are taking pictures of the aeroplane carrying the camera, the necessary depth of field can be worked out in advance, and you can choose the stop to suit. Remember, however, that you might want the background in focus too — nice, sharp clouds or ground details can add some useful drama.

If you are setting up for an air-to-air shoot, life is more difficult. You will need plenty of depth to make sure the subject aircraft is sharp, as you are shooting blind. This shouldn't be too much of a problem as you will be using a standard or wide lens.

FEEDBACK

One problem is feedback — or rather, lack of it. When you've got a camera pressed to your face, you know it has fired because of the noise and vibration. With the camera outside a noisy aircraft cabin you simply don't have these clues.

If the camera is still in view from your seat, put a small piece of reflective tape on the top of the rewind knob. A piece the size and shape of the fold-out crank should do. This will provide visual confirmation that the film is at least being wound through the camera.

Many motordrives have lights which flash when a frame is fired. These are often linked to the film sprocket, and so again give positive proof that the film is winding, although they are usually positioned on the rear of the motordrive and so will usually be out of sight. If you can see into the lens, you can watch for the lens aperture closing.

FRAMING

Undoubtedly, the greatest difficulty with remote photography is knowing what is in the frame at any given time. The situation isn't too bad if you are shooting the outside of your own aircraft — all the framing can be done on the ground before you fly, and all you have to do is try to work out what (if anything) is in the background.

In all other cases, you need to get to know your equipment really well. Stick to one lens, and use it a lot until you have a good intuitive feel for its angle of view. When you install the camera, see if there is anything you can use as a sight — a distant landmark for ground-based cameras, or perhaps the tail of your aircraft for air-to-air shots.

If you have more than one stab at the sortie, you could try shooting instant film — Polaroid makes 35 mm film — on the first trip, processing it on the ground to check that your aim is good, and the equipment is functioning. If there is only one chance, you could still try shooting some test shots with the aircraft on the ground.

If the background is likely to form an important part of the shot — in air-to-air and pilot pictures, for example — you can get a good idea of what will appear in the frame by flying one pass in the opposite direction to the picture-taking run. On that pass, everything you see ahead of you will appear in the background once you turn around and start taking pictures.

PRE-FLIGHT CHECKS

The flight might be a one-off, or it might be costing you a lot of money, so you want it to be right. The last thing you need is an equipment malfunction. Before loading the film, and with the back open, fire the motor a few times, checking that the film sprocket and take-up spool are turning and that the shutter is firing. Holding the camera up to a bright object or patch of light will help you to see if the shutter is opening properly — at least, it will give you a rough idea and reveal any serious problems. It is also worth checking the meter against another camera, or a hand-held meter.

Fire the motor through a long sequence, checking the speed to make sure the batteries are not on the verge of dying. If in any doubt, load a completely new set of batteries; they are much cheaper than another flight, even supposing you can repeat the event. Batteries don't work quite so well in low temperatures, and up at a few thousand feet with the slipstream screaming past, the temperature can drop very low indeed. If the camera is out on the wing, making sure it's well wrapped up, and that air is not moving directly across the camera bottom (where the battery is usually located) will help. Some cameras allow you to remove the battery and place it in a small container, which is connected by a cable to the camera. This is designed for arctic conditions — the battery compartment is placed inside the photographer's clothes and kept warm by body heat. This may be one solution to your problem, if the connecting cable is long enough. By the same token, it's not a bad idea for you to dress warmly too. If you're not used to this sort of flying, get the pilot's advice about the best clothes for the aeroplane in those weather conditions.

Once you are on the ground again, take the film out and repeat the pre-take-off checks, to make sure that everything is still functioning.

LIGHTING

As most of your photography will be outdoors, with your subjects some distance away, good flash technique would seem an unnecessary skill. Yet it is surprising how often a flashgun will improve a shot, or even allow you to do something you thought was impossible.

In a hangar or museum, or even outdoors when the sun has set, you can light whole aircraft using studio flash units. The techniques are the same as lighting a car, a statue or even a building, and we will leave them to the technical photography manuals. But even with more modest shots, a small flashgun can help out, although before we get on to the benefits and techniques, let's look at a couple of the limitations and pitfalls.

The use of flash is equated, in some people's minds, with being indoors. Whatever the light level, there are people who will stick flash units on their cameras as soon as there is a roof over their heads. Quite often it simply isn't necessary. Even more often it is a positive barrier to getting a decent photograph.

Sometimes the thing that has drawn you to a subject is the lighting (although you don't necessarily realise this immediately).

There are degrees of backlighting other than direct into-sun silhouettes. Partial backlighting, using reflections and highlights to pick up details, is good for mood

Letting off a flashgun destroys the original lighting effect and thus destroys your reason for taking the shot. At other times, the subject is just too far away to light adequately with flash. Trying to illuminate a B-17 bomber in a dark hangar or museum with an average camera-mounted flashgun is a triumph of optimism over technical expertise. Few flashguns — with the exception of studio or large professional units — are very valuable at distances of more than three or four metres.

There are two ways you might use flash: as your main light source when there isn't enough ambient illumination, and as a secondary light source to improve your shots. The first is straightforward, and is largely a matter of reading the manual that came with your flashgun to get the right exposure. There are some subjects which don't take to flash lighting very well — objects behind glass or with shiny surfaces will reflect the flash light like a mirror, giving a glaring highlight in the shot and fooling any automatic exposure system into under-exposure. This can be cured in most cases by putting the flash off to one side, but it's something that has to be borne in mind.

Unless you are carting around vast amounts of studio lighting, this approach will be limited to fairly close, small objects. Exactly how close depends on the power of the flash unit you're using, but the average pocketable unit will prove useful with subjects up to three or four metres away. Museum exhibits, such as engines and aircraft details, may benefit from some portable illumination, as will shooting in cockpits.

Silhouettes work best if the shape is simple and strong

When using flash as your main light source, watch for excessive illumination in the foreground. The closer they are to the flashgun, the brighter objects are lit. This can result in over-exposed and distracting foreground objects, the ground being a common culprit. Tilting the flashgun upwards slightly reduces the risk.

You can use flash for air-to-air shots, providing you have a sufficiently powerful unit. This is not as distracting for the pilots as you might think, although it might cause a few hearts to race among unsuspecting people on the ground. However, it's tricky, as exposure is difficult to judge, and the light is rarely flattering to the aircraft.

The second approach to flash is perhaps more useful. By mixing in some flash with the existing lighting, a technique known as fill-in flash, you can improve the technical quality of your shot. The brief duration of the flash light is like using a fast shutter speed, and will sharpen-up hand-held shots. The light from the flashgun is also the right colour — photographic 'daylight' — and so will clean up the colour of shots taken under artificial illumination, such as tungsten or fluorescent lamps.

The simplest way of mixing lighting in this way is to do a 50/50 split. Start by working out the correct stop for your flashgun. You can use the guide number principle — dividing the guide number (for a given film speed) by the distance gives the f-stop. More often, in these days of 'computerized' flashguns, you will switch to one of the automatic settings, and will be told which stop to use. Let's say you have set the flashgun to its f5.6 setting.

Now you forget about flash for a minute, and work out the correct exposure using the available light, with the lens set to f5.6. The resulting shutter speed must be at or slower than the camera's flash synchronization speed (typically 1/60th or 1/125th). If this isn't the case, choose another setting on the flashgun which gives a smaller stop and repeat the process. Set the shutter speed on the camera.

You now effectively have two light sources, each of which would give a correct exposure with the lens set to f5.6. Using both of them together means you have twice the amount of light you need, and the picture would be over-exposed by one stop — so you now stop down the lens (you do *not* adjust the shutter speed as this affects only the available light exposure) by one stop, to f8. When you shoot at these settings you wind up with a picture in which both flash and available light have contributed equally.

Evening light is naturally warm and soft. An 81A amber filter can be used to enhance the effect, but might be overdoing it

It's worth experimenting with other proportions between the two light sources. For example, if you are shooting a subject with lots of shadows (and this applies outdoors as well as in) you can set the normal exposure for the highlights and use a little flash to put detail into the shadows. If your available light exposure gives you an aperture of f8, you could set the auto exposure on the flashgun to f4 or even f2.8. The resulting flashlight will be far too weak to affect the sunlit areas, but will help pick up bits of the subject lurking in darkness.

There are times when the two light sources might illuminate completely different parts of the scene. In a cockpit, for example, the view through the window might be sunlit while the instrument panel and general interior is in deep shadow. In this case you would set the exposure for the daylight and then select a setting on the flashgun to give the same aperture, or perhaps a half to one stop down to slightly under-expose the interior — this prevents it looking artificial. In this case, as the two light sources are not mixing, you would not bother to close down by one stop.

It should be repeated that the shutter speed must never get shorter than the camera's flash sync speed. In addition, these techniques are easiest with ordinary automatic flashguns — the type that integrate with the camera's metering system are difficult to subvert in this way.

The more normal source of light is the sun, but even here there are various ways of using the light. For a start, think about the angle of the lighting. With the sun over your shoulder, you will get an even illumination across the aircraft, which is good for showing markings and so on, although you might have a few problems with bright highlights as the sun is reflected in glossy panels and canopies. Side lighting shows up rivets and surface detail nicely. You may get a problem with prop blades and struts casting shadows, but on the whole this kind of light can be highly effective.

Aircraft landing lights can provide useful highlights, especially when the weather is overcast

If the subject is backlit you may wind up with nothing more than a silhouette. Increasing the exposure to get more detail in the aircraft will soon result in the background burning out. The decision is yours, but bear in mind that backlighting can still be effective, especially if the outline of the aircraft is an instantly recognisable one — the Spitfire springs to mind here. The sun glaring through the canopy can be highly dramatic.

Choosing the right time of day is important. Many of the best air-to-air shots have been taken early in the morning or late evening. When the sun is low you get a nice sidelight which is also quite warm in colour, and clouds and background landscapes are beautifully lit. Of course, that's if you're lucky enough to get a choice about when you shoot, but it's worth keeping in mind if you're planning a photo session. The same applies to aircraft on the ground, too. And aircraft on final approach to landing are often best shot near twilight when their landing lights become more visible and dramatic.

Left: Artificial lighting creates colour casts. Here, mixed tungsten and fluorescent lighting gives amber and green casts respectively. This mixed lighting source is impossible to correct with filters, but pictorially one kind of lighting tends to cancel or balance the other anyway

Right: Flash can be useful to fill in details, especially in cockpits

You might not have much in the way of sun at all. Yet you shouldn't despair just because there are clouds; indeed, an overcast day, with its flatter, more even light, can make your job easier. You may have to open up a stop or two, or use faster film, and you might want to use an 81A light amber filter to warm up colours, if you're shooting on colour stock.

PROFILE:
NORMAL PEALING

Slick shots of gleaming airliners cruising through fluffy clouds are the speciality of UK photographer Normal Pealing. Something of a rarity, being one of the few professionals to work in both movie and stills, this Surrey-based film-maker and photographer operates from an office at Fairoaks Airport, near Woking, shooting pictures and film footage for airlines and aircraft manufacturers.

Although he has always had a passion for photography, Norman's professional background is in film-making. He came out of the Royal Air Force and joined the British Aircraft Corporation (as it was then) in 1965, staying eighteen years to make sales publicity films, until eventually setting up his own company in 1983. At BAC he was involved in all the company's products — guided weapons, space and military and civil aviation. Since branching out on his own he has concentrated largely on civil aircraft, and has increased the amount of time he spends taking photographs. He now has air-to-air film and pictures of around 150 aircraft types.

'I took the odd stills for BAC, but it wasn't part of the job really. It happened now and then because it's difficult to get both a cine photographer and a stills photographer in the back of a Jaguar or Harrier!' Now things are somewhat different: 'Time-wise, it's probably about 70 per cent stills, 30 per cent film-making.'

Although his pictures turn up in books and magazines around the world, most of the pictures are shot for the airlines and manufacturers. For example, he does all the photography and film-making for SAAB on the 340 programme and has also been working on the more recent Saab 2000.

A lot of Norman's work consists of selling pictures to corporates — airlines and aircraft manufacturers who want to include pictures with their press releases, have photographs on their walls and exhibition stands, and generally use the shots for promotional purposes. As the final result is frequently a photographic print (as opposed to a mechanically reproduced picture) it makes sense to shoot on negative film, as getting prints this way is cheaper and easier than going from transparency. When he gets a client who needs a transparency for reproduction — for books or magazines — he gets a tranny made from the negative. He very rarely shoots in black and white, preferring to convert from colour. That way he keeps his options open.

Also slightly unusual, considering much of his work is hand-held air-to-air shots, is the fact that Norman uses medium format. His standard camera is a Hasselblad, usually fitted with a motordrive. To this he adds normal and wide angle lenses — which, for medium format cameras, are 80 mm and 50 mm – for air-to-air work. Occasionally he might switch to a 150 mm, but would rather have the subject aircraft close enough so that he didn't have to: 'I insist that at least one of the pilots is used to formation flying — all the better if both of them are. But sometimes you find a pilot who isn't used to it will keep his distance. I've still got to get reasonable pictures so I use a longer lens, but try not to if possible.'

For ground-to-air shots he goes up to 350 mm and 500 mm, which are equivalent to 200 mm and 300 mm on 35 mm cameras. If this doesn't do the job, he adds a 2x teleconverter to boost the lenses to 700 mm and 1000 mm. Although not a Hasselblad units, he rates the converter very highly: 'I've looked at contact sheets and forgotten which ones I used the converter on, the results are that good. The only trouble is that you lose speed.'

A few times he has strapped cameras to aircraft, and that's when he switches to 35 mm, as the medium format gear is too bulky. But he prefers using his cameras hand-held: 'I like to see in the viewfinder what I'm getting, but obviously there are some cracking shots you can get with a remote camera, especially if you've got a video assist, with a video camera looking at the focusing screen, and sharing the same view.'

All the gear is stock equipment, and he likes to keep it simple. 'I tend not to use filters. On an air-to-air session, the last thing you want to do is to start worrying about what filter you have on and what effect it is having — meantime the shot's gone. If there's anything you want to do afterwards you can do it at the printing stage.'

The technique is pretty straightforward, too. His main concern is avoiding problems with vibration and turbulence. 'One's always trying to get the fastest speed, which on a Hasselblad is 1/500th. Any faster would stop the prop, especially on a modern turbo-prop where they're spinning slightly slower anyway. You have to try not to freeze the propeller because it looks a bit silly.'

Showing what can be done in a short time, this shot of a Beech Duke is one from a session that took just fifteen minutes from wheels-up to landing. Fill-in flash helped the rapidly failing light

Opposite: The RAF's Red Arrows display team is invariably photogenic, but this shot really captures the grace of this outstanding outfit. Shot from the back seat of another Hawk aircraft, the elegant composition disguises the hard work Norman put into it. If you turn the page so that the formation is horizontal, you'll get a better idea of how it actually looked through the viewfinder, as the camera-ship looped with the formation

An Airbus A320 hangs everything in the breeze to keep station behind the much slower camera ship. In this case it works well, as Norman has made the most of the sun and landing lights

Opposite: When photographing an aircraft in airline livery, Norman likes to get a suitable background. TAN is an Argentinian regional airline, and for this shot of a Saab 340 Norman chose the Andes for his backdrop. Taking out half the door from a Piper Navajo gave him a good view unobstructed by glass, but the altitude of 14,500 feet made it cold work, and breathing wasn't too easy either

Norman finds that shooting through glass is a problem, so he avoids it whenever possible — which is most of the time. 'I try not to shoot through glass. Normally one would try to have a door off or a window off.'

That's sometimes easier said that done. Getting the right camera ship is part of Norman's skill. The main consideration is that it has to be compatible with what you're trying to shoot, while still providing adequate viewing for the photographer.

'There's no one ideal aeroplane — it depends on the shot you want. A B-25 is useful, but you have to do a lot of climbing around to get from one end to the other. You've got this speed barrier of 160 knots. It's difficult to find an aircraft that will do a bit more where you can have the door off. You start getting into pressurized aeroplanes. You can probably creep it up to 170, 180 knots, but with airliners at that speed they're going to be flying around with flaps and slats and who knows what dangling about. At best you can probably get away with a little bit of flap, which you might not notice.'

He's shot DC-10s and 747s from an Aztec, but in the case of one Jumbo session, the set-up was less than ideal. 'The 747 was flying through, which isn't always terribly useful. You get the shot, perhaps three or four shots, but that's it. It's go-around time and there's a lot of valuable time wasted.'

And it's not just getting the right type of chase aircraft. Getting hold of any sort of aeroplane can be a hassle. And when he does find it, he has to get it into the air at the same time as his subject, which can be a headache. When he goes to the US he hires an aircraft for the time he's over there, getting friends and colleagues to fly it. That way, he knows he has a camera ship. At home, there are three companies at Fairoaks Airport which he uses regularly, so he not only increases his chances of having an aeroplane available, but builds up a useful relationship with the pilots who know his way of working and what he wants.

By law, photo sessions cannot use aircraft carrying fare-paying passengers. But at the same time, it is extremely expensive for an airline or manufacturer to put an aircraft in the air just for a photo session. One's always conscious of the time you're taking — it's costing someone a lot of money. You want to try to get as much in the can as quickly as possible. They normally write it off as crew training. A lot depends on the airline — how much of a

budget they've got. If you get an hour you think you're lucky. But sometimes if you get a long time it can be embarrassing, trying to think what to do next. You're used to getting the shots you need, and so you can do it quickly.'

Sometimes he can bend things a little. With SAAB, the reason for shooting the aircraft is usually that it is the first for a new customer, and so the first of that model in a new livery. SAAB needs shots for press releases and promotional material. But the aircraft may be in the country for just a short time, and the only chance Norman might get to shoot it in the air is when it is on the way home to Sweden — and that could happen at night. ('I have used fill-in flash on air-to-air shots occasionally. You can do it if you're close enough.') The solution is often to wait until the aircraft has been delivered to the customer.

'We normally go and visit the airline anyway — spend a few days with them, fly round their routes. We can normally get the aircraft up for half an hour, and it's nice to get the aircraft over its own territory anyway.'

Going abroad to shoot the aeroplane can solve Norman's biggest problem: 'In England it's the weather! You can't lay anything on. In the States you can practically guarantee good weather, or if it's bad weather, it's usually "interesting" bad weather. But over here it's claggy, and if you go above it, it's probably flat and horrible. It's nice if you can get up among some cu-nims.'

Apart from setting the aircraft against a suitable national backdrop, the choice of scenery is important to the shot. 'I like to think I take pictures of aeroplanes, rather than just photographs of them. Instead of just a side-on shot counting all the rivets, I try to get something interesting, make it look like a picture. Sometimes you don't get the option of what you have in the background. We try to fly a racetrack pattern to vary it, and to get a change of light at each end.'

Most of the session is worked out on the ground beforehand. Norman is occasionally in contact with the pilot of the subject aircraft, either through a hand-held transceiver or through his aircraft's radio. But this can waste time when the frequencies are busy. Most of the time, however, he relies on hand signals, if the other aircraft is reasonably close, and a good ground briefing.

Norman is not a pilot himself, but years working in the business have given him an excellent understanding of the problems, the techniques and the language of flying. And he listens to what pilots have to say. 'On air-to-air it's really the pilots who are doing it. All I'm doing is taking the pictures. It's their skill in putting the aeroplanes in the position you want them in. At a briefing, the easiest thing is to tell them what you want, and they'll tell you whether they can do it or not. If they can't do it then that's it. It's essential for them to know what you're trying to get.'

Sometimes the customers specify what they want — some special feature or equipment they want to highlight, or hide.

Most of the time, however, the choice of how to portray the aircraft is up to Norman. They rely not just on his skill, but his enthusiasm. He often takes pictures purely for himself, because aircraft are a passion as well as a job, which is one reason why his office is at an airport. 'I like being on an active airfield — I like hearing aircraft buzz around.'

This close-up shot shows off the Saab 340's excellent cockpit visibility — even from the outside. But keeping formation at close range requires high class flying. Fortunately, Norman had the services of Saab's chief test pilot, Per Pellerbergs

IN PRACTICE

AIR SHOWS

For the aviation photographer, turning up at a decent air show is like being a child let loose in a toy shop. There is a rush of excitement as you begin to spot all those rare and beautiful machines, soon followed by the realization that there is so much to do in a limited time. However, by following a few basic survival tips, you can make your visit both more productive and less tiring.

Air shows are well attended by photogenic aerobatic teams. Formation teams like this one take up more of the sky than single aircraft and so fill the frame better even if you don't have very long lenses

Get there early, but don't plan on leaving early. Typically, air shows open their doors at 0800 or 0900, although the flying doesn't start until 1200. All the same, it is worth getting there when the gates first open. You will be able to park more easily. You can have a leisurely stroll, examining the static exhibits which are already there, photographing those aircraft still arriving, selecting the best spot on the crowd line, and locating the essential facilities — food stalls, toilets and bar, not necessarily in that order. You can get a lot of the best static shots before the worst of the crowds arrive. And you can shop for souvenirs in greater comfort.

Leaving is a different story. Don't jump into your car and make a rush for the gate; around 50,000 other people will have had the same idea. Get some more static shots, including pictures of the late arrivals or departures. As it's likely to be late in the day, you should be treated to a nice warm, low sun, so make sure you've saved some film — always keep a roll back. Admire your purchases. Sort out your, by now, untidy camera bag. Clean your equipment. And give it about an hour before making your exit.

Shows often give you opportunities to get shots of military hardware that is otherwise hard to find or get close to

For the display itself, plan the best place on the crowd line, which usually means having a clear field of view. Watch out for tannoys, parked cars and other obstacles placed in front of the crowd line. They are easy to miss when you first pick your place, but have a habit of creeping into your pictures as you pan with the aircraft. Take a good look at the background, too — indeed, anything which is likely to come into shot.

Watch the crowd line, too. When it starts to fill, grab your place and hang on to it. This is a situation in which taking along a spouse, friend or member of the family comes in handy — he or she can reserve your place while you carry on walking around, shooting pictures of the static displays. By this time, the luckless partner is usually so fed up with peering into yet another engine cowling that he or she is only too pleased to be able to sit down and read a book or fall asleep.

Getting close to the main hospitality areas is usually a shrewd move. The President's or organizer's tent is usually the focus for the aerobatic displays, especially if they are being judged for competitions. Alternatively, watch the aircraft taking off, and position yourself in line with the point where they rotate — that is, where they point the nose upwards just before leaving the ground. This can yield exciting pictures of aircraft airborne but with some background detail.

Take a bit of time to research the event. Don't be shy of asking the organizers where parachutists will land, where special events will take place and what the actual running order of events is likely to be — most printed programmes are, at best, extremely optimistic and, at worst, works of total fiction. They are printed days or weeks before the event, and as aircraft drop out and others take their place, the show can change a great deal.

It should be possible to deduce the habits of most of the aircraft. Find out which is the active runway: most aircraft will line up around about the same spot at the downwind end for their take-off runs. And run-up points or turning circles are good places to catch aircraft.

Knowing when to expect things is invaluable. For example, if you know that a Harrier is about to come along, you might want to make sure you have at least half a roll of film, so that you don't wind up changing film during the best parts of the routine. Or you might want to have a particular lens in place, or move to a more advantageous position.

Don't weigh yourself down. A good supply of cold drinks and snacks can be a blessing when you've been sitting in the sun for a couple of hours. But it becomes an almost intolerable burden when you have to lug around a coolbox on top of your camera gear. It's liable to make you pass up shots just because it seems too much effort to rearrange the stuff. Anything that makes you miss pictures is bad news. Yet again, an assistant, in the form of spouse, family member or friend, is invaluable for guarding the stuff while you are off taking pictures.

Ground crews and equipment shouldn't be necessarily regarded as unwanted intrusions. Try to use them to add to the interest of the photograph

Bring plenty of money. Apart from the inevitable hot dogs, ice creams and souvenirs, you are highly likely to run out of film. It is easy to underestimate the amount of film you can get through on these occasions. The good news is that there are invariably vendors of film at the show. The bad news is that they have every type of film Kodak, Fuji and/or Agfa make — except the one you use.

If you find that shooting static aircraft is a problem — because there are too many people around them; they have ugly covers thrown over them; they are festooned with 'Remove Before Flight' tags and tie-down ropes, or they have nasty power pylons sprouting behind them — then wait a while. You may find the aircraft you want to shoot are destined to appear in the display, and a little basic research, such as looking in the programme, might confirm this. The aeroplanes will be much easier to shoot as they taxi past, and will also be in flight configuration, which includes having a pilot stuck in the cockpit.

It is also useful to turn up the day before the show and/or the day after, particularly if it is a big event involving the movement of many aircraft. There is a better chance of getting close to the aircraft and talking to their owners, and you can get shots of aircraft arriving and departing.

During the show days there are frequent opportunities to ride in some of the exhibits, as owners try to defray their costs by running pleasure flights. This might even present air-to-air opportunities, albeit out of your control.

Choosing lenses for an air show depends very much on the specific circumstances. However, to get flying aircraft you will almost certainly find a 200 mm lens useful for the larger machines, while you may have to go up to 300 mm and 400 mm to shoot individual fighters. The 200 mm will also be useful for some formation teams, although large groups of aircraft, including military teams like the Red Arrows or Thunderbirds, may force you to use a 100 mm lens, or thereabouts, to get the whole group in at close range. The longer lenses will still be useful for pulling out single aircraft.

Sometimes it's impossible to avoid some peripheral clutter. But it can be used to good effect by adding interest to the shot

While on the subject of display teams, anticipation is everything. Listen to the announcer, who often gives a running commentary on the manoeuvre you are about to see. When shooting groups, try to shoot when the sun is on the side of the aircraft facing you, as teams are often identified as much by their colours and markings as by the aircraft they fly. And when faced with aircraft moving in different directions, decide which is the more important and pan with that. For example, when two aircraft cross in opposite directions in front of the crowd, it is better to pan with one aircraft — making it sharp but the other aircraft very blurred, giving a tremendous impression of speed — than to try to stop the camera and get both sharp. What you will actually get is *two* blurred aircraft.

GETTING RID OF CROWDS

There is one common problem which plagues photographers at shows and museums: other people. Short of mass genocide, or creating an ugly scene, there is little you can do about getting rid of intruders other than bide your time. Patience is a virtue of inestimable value to any photographer.

Although curing the problem is difficult, you can take steps to avoid it. This often comes down to choosing the right time of day (or season, in the case of museums).

At air shows, getting there before most of the crowds arrive, and waiting around until they have left, are the best ways of keeping the hordes out of your pictures. There is one slight hitch, which is that many display aircraft are at the field for only a brief period, and may not be around when you want them. There is little you can do about this, unless the show runs over several days. If, for example, the show is on two consecutive days, it is quite likely that many of the aircraft will stay overnight at the field. That means you stand a better chance of getting the ones you want at the end of the first day, and with luck, you'll have a nice low sun casting a warm light over the aircraft.

Museums are less likely to be full of screaming schoolkids if you go during the week and/or early in the morning. In other words, choose the off-peak hours. It's also worth inquiring if you can obtain special permission to come in when the museum is normally closed to the public.

If it looks as though crowds are inevitable, try getting in close. Putting a wide angle lens on your camera and getting up near the aircraft should put most, if not all, of the crowd behind you. It has the bonus of moving any intrusive barriers out of your picture, too, as you are likely to be leaning over them!

SAFETY

It is a little unusual to talk about safety in a photography book. Cameras are not noted as dangerous objects: aircraft, on the other hand, are, and playing with them can be a hazardous occupation.

There are obvious problems, like getting chopped into hamburger meat by propeller blades or sucked into jet intakes. Unfortunately, the dangers are all too easy to dismiss. After all, you would hear a prop plane coming towards you, wouldn't you?

Well, no. You'd be surprised how easy it is for even a big, growling monster like a Bearcat to sneak up behind you. For one thing, there is always a lot of ambient noise at airfields, especially on busy display days. And unless your ears point backwards, hearing is biased towards the front — as is your concentration as you focus on the subject ahead of you. When you're peering through the camera, the only part of the world that you're really conscious of is the bit in the viewfinder.

At an air show, it is unlikely that you will be allowed to mix with the aeroplanes, unless you have sought special permission, or have tagged along with one of the display teams. However, at a small airfield it is quite easy to walk on to the ramp.

The main rule is to avoid daydreaming. If you step backwards to improve your shot, *always* take a look behind you first — a good look. And at all times, keep looking around to see if anything is approaching.

If you are near a prop-driven aircraft which has its engine running, keep one eye on the prop at all times. Keep watching the crew members for warnings or signs that the aircraft might be about to move. If it is a conventional design, with the fan at the front, stay behind the wing — although that can have problems too, as the prop wash during an engine run-up can easily bowl

Below (left): When you can't get a decent overall shot, go for details. (Right): Photographs are an excellent way of recording information, particularly when it's supplied free on the side of the aircraft

you over. If you must go around the front, keep well away from the aircraft. And if you need to be near, stay within arm's distance of the wing's leading edge. It's not a bad idea to continually touch it. This will usually keep you safely away from the meat slicer.

Jets are dangerous at both ends. At the front, engine air intakes are capable of sucking you in, invariably causing severe engine damage — although you won't be around to worry about that. At the back, the hot blast can leave you feeling pretty uncomfortable, too, even from some distance away. If you should happen to be near a jet when you hear the engines winding up, move well away.

With jets, you can also pose a serious safety problem to the crew if you are careless with your belongings. Discarded film cans, dropped lens brushes and other small items are easily sucked into the engines where they can cause expensive Foreign Object Damage (FOD). This term has been adopted to describe the objects themselves and you will find FOD cans — rubbish bins — in hangars and on ramps at all military and many civilian

Below: Static displays are often difficult to photograph well — both backgrounds and foregrounds frequently have unwanted clutter

Above: It's often better to wait for the aircraft to taxi or be towed out

fields. Military ground crews perform 'FOD sweeps' before flying starts, to ensure there is no rubbish lying around the ramp or runway. And on most flightlines, ordinary headgear is banned, as it tends to fly off in the breeze. Use the FOD bins for your rubbish. Pick up potential FOD even if it isn't yours. And make sure you aren't carrying anything which is likely to fly away or you could end up having to buy the air force or airline a new aeroplane.

It has to be said that the aeroplanes themselves are less considerate. Prop and jet aircraft will savagely kick up all sorts of grit and rubbish and throw it at you, should you be foolish enough to stand behind the aeroplane. Often it will be mixed with leaking oil, especially if the aircraft is an ageing warbird. This flying debris can damage both you and your equipment, and is best avoided.

Perhaps the most common, and insidious, injury caused by aircraft is to your ears. Everyone knows that aircraft are noisy, but few appreciate how damaging that racket can be. With a propeller aircraft, most of the noise is caused by the prop itself, as it tears the air apart. So the most docile-looking planes can be the most lethal if they have fast props with tips that go supersonic.

That's not to underestimate the noise of the engine. You don't have to stand for long beside a V-12 Merlin to appreciate that some form of ear protection is probably a good idea. And getting close to a jet will convert you instantly. You might *like* the sound of aircraft — and there are few sounds more thrilling than the growl and whine of well-tuned aero engines. But even relatively short exposure to high noise levels can cause permanent damage. And it can be hard to concentrate on your photography with your eardrums rattling painfully.

You needn't worry if you spend all your time on the crowd line at air shows as you will be a safe distance from the offending machines. If you are the guest of the military they will normally insist that you wear ear protection — and supply it, too. Otherwise, it's down to you. A set of headphone-like ear defenders can be picked up quite cheaply from hardware stores, where they are sold to chainsaw-wielding handymen. If you don't want something that bulky, small, malleable earplugs — the type you scrunch up, stick in your ears and wait for them to expand — work very well. The one caveat about using ear protection is that you have to be even more alert, and use your eyes more, if you are to avoid walking into aeroplanes.

Finally, always obey instructions. If someone tells you not to stand in a certain place, he or she probably has a good reason. Likewise, if you are asked to move away from an aircraft, do so immediately, or you could be endangering yourself and other people. A little common sense and a lot of awareness of what is going on around you, should help prolong your photographic career and your life expectancy.

WHAT TO DO WITH YOUR PICTURES

What do you do with your pictures once you've taken them? That's a tough one. How many times have you been asked just why you take pictures, and been stuck for an adequate answer?

This is not a difficult question for everybody, of course. Some people have very clear ideas on why they take pictures of aeroplanes, and we touched on some of them in the introduction. You might be a professional, someone whose primary interest is in aircraft, and whose interest in photography is simply a way of expanding or documenting that activity, or an aircraft owner wanting shots of your machine.

Whatever your reasons for taking photographs, you will soon end up with a large, and ever expanding, collection of pictures, and the day will come when you realize you need to do something about it.

Your first thought, if they are prints, might be to stick the pictures in an album. But there could be a more lucrative use for them. Having invested a lot of time and money in taking the pictures, it would be nice to get something back. If you are a professional, then you are already doing it. If you are shooting the pictures for a specific purpose — promotional use, perhaps — then your reward is in a job well done. But what if you are shooting purely for pleasure? The cost of equipment and film can quickly mount up. Selling a few pictures is a good way of subsidizing your hobby — and who knows, you might even discover a new career.

Try to get a vantage point that provides an attractive background for taxying aircraft

There are two main ways of selling pictures. You can sell actual prints to people who want to put them on their walls, or you can go for the more profitable approach, selling pictures for publication in magazines and books, and perhaps as postcards and posters.

However, before we get on to where to send your pictures, let's look at *how* to send them. With black and white pictures, a 10 x 8 inch print is best. This should not be mounted or framed in any way, nor should it be heavily cropped. Never send negatives. With colour shots, transparencies are preferred as they give superior reproduction and are easier to scan — the process that turns the original into the colour separations needed for the printing process.

Always use sturdy packaging. Padded envelopes with some thick card inserted for stiffening are ideal. Hand delivering the pictures is safest, but if you post them, make sure you use a system which provides proof of delivery. Include a note with the pictures stating what the contents are, what they are for, and who you are. Never, ever send transparencies in glass mounts. No matter how good the packaging you stand a better than 50/50 chance of having some of the glass shatter, usually doing irreparable damage to the pictures — not to mention your client's hands when the pictures are pulled from the envelope.

Even with the greatest care, pictures do wear out. Every time a picture goes through the reproduction process it gets a little more dog-eared. It is not unknown for transparencies to come back with fingerprints on them, and for pictures to be damaged or lost completely. With prints this is no problem as you can always do some more, but with transparencies it is an important consideration. If you have a particularly good shot, which you think might make repeat sales, get some high quality duplicates made. To avoid too much loss of quality, the dupe should be on a larger format than the original. For example, if the original is a 35 mm transparency it's a good idea to have a 5 x 4 inch dupe. If the customer does not mind working from a dupe, send that. But even if you have to send out the original, you still have the dupe as a back-up in case of emergencies.

If a picture is irreparably damaged or lost while it is in the care of a client, that client is responsible for compensating you. If it is a print, the amount comes to the cost of replacing the print. If it is an original transparency, the amount should take into consideration lost future revenues. Trade organizations, such as the British Association of Picture Libraries and Agencies (BAPLA) and the American Society of Magazine Photographers (ASMP) in the US, set standard rates for loss fees. They can be contacted at the following addresses:

BAPLA
13 Woodberry Crescent
London N10 1PJ
Tel: 01-883 2351
Fax: 01-883 9215

ASMP
419 Park Avenue South
New York, NY 10016
Tel: (212) 889-9144

MAGAZINES

Aviation magazines are often able to use pictures by amateurs. If you have taken pictures of an event or show — particularly one abroad — or have some unusual shots that might be of general interest, ring the editor first to see if he or she might want to use them. Sometimes you will be invited to come in and show the work, but more often you will be asked to send in a selection of pictures. Around five to ten shots will give the editor a good idea of the quality of your work, but make sure you send a covering note pointing out what other shots you have. It is a good idea to send a stamped, addressed envelope with your submission: by reducing the editor's workload you will win points and ensure a speedier return of the pictures should they turn out to be unusable.

Don't be too disheartened by rejection: it's not necessarily a value judgment on your work. The chances are that the magazine simply doesn't have a suitable slot for your pictures.

BOOKS

Books are tougher to get into than magazines. You need a strong theme and the quality of photography tends to be higher. Most publishers will consider speculative suggestions, but don't bother to write the text until you have a firm commitment. A two-page synopsis, a sample selection of pictures and — if the book is to contain a reasonable amount of text — a sample chapter are what you need for your initial submission.

Before submitting material to a publisher, go down to a well-stocked bookshop and carry out a quick market survey. A perusal of the shelves will tell you which publishers cover aviation, and the type of books they do. There's little point in sending an idea for an aviation book to a publisher who doesn't work in that field.

Below (left): When deciding where to park yourself, select a point on the crowd line where the aircraft rotate, for more interesting shots

Your best bet, if you have a good selection of pictures on a single theme, is to go for the highly-illustrated, picture book market. To give you an idea, a full-colour picture book will typically have up to 120 pictures. To give the editor a reasonable choice you will need to provide at least 500 top quality shots, with plenty of variation, which will probably have been culled from 1,000–1,500 original pictures (not including the duff ones).

A slightly less ambitious approach is to go for the postcard, calendar and poster markets. Again, a search through the shops and trade publications, should turn up potential clients.

Above: Save some film for the end of the day. It is then generally less crowded and the light, from a low sun, is often better than during the show

PICTURE LIBRARIES

You can escape the hard grind of trying to sell your pictures by putting them into a photo library. These businesses carry large stocks of pictures, usually by several photographers, and have the kind of contacts in the publishing and advertising industries that most individuals could never hope to develop.

Most libraries have one or more specialist subjects, and you stand a better chance of selling your photographs if you put them with a library known for aviation pictures. Picture editors and researchers, art buyers and anyone else in the market for aeroplane photographs, will go to that kind of library first.

Your pictures have to be good quality, and you need a large number of them. Some libraries demand a minimum initial submission of 2,000 pictures. Others will accept less, but will expect you to build up a larger stock quite quickly. And this makes sense: you are competing with the other pictures in the library, and the more photographs you have, the better chance you stand of having yours sold.

Although some libraries do handle black and white pictures, they are normally archive or news photos. The vast majority demand colour transparencies, and some still cling to an outmoded bias towards medium and large format, although they will rarely turn down high quality 35 mm stuff. Your photographs should all be fully labelled, which we'll come to in a minute.

The library handles all the business aspects — promotion, submission, billing and so on. In effect, your job ends when you send the pictures in. All you have to do then is wait for the money to roll in. The library's cut is normally fifty per cent of the fee, although some take sixty per cent. In return, the library will normally expect you to leave the photographs with them for a stated minimum period — typically two or three years.

If you have a large stock of good quality pictures, you could set up your own library. The stock does have to be *very* large, however. To stand a chance of selling a decent number of photographs you have to send out ten, twenty or thirty times that number. A minimum stock would be 20,000 photographs, but that's just a start. Large libraries have millions of pictures. And selling stock pictures is a full-time job. To find suitable photo libraries, look in some of the trade directories, such as *The Picture Researcher's Handbook, The Creative Handbook, The Black Book* and so on. Your local lending library should be able to help with these.

PRINTS

Selling your pictures as works of art to adorn the walls of the astute and the enlightened is, on the face of it, a much simpler way of squeezing money out of your hobby. To do it on a large, scale, however, you need retail outlets and some money to finance your initial stock. You could try mail order, which at least means you can do it all yourself, but it can turn into a full-time job. And you have to come up with the money for advertising before you (hopefully) start taking orders. Yet none of these drawbacks applies if you simply want to sell to friends and acquaintances, and while you won't get rich that way, you will defray some of your expenses.

LABELLING

Whatever you intend to do with the pictures, it's essential to properly label or identify them. It is all too easy to convince yourself that you will be able to remember what the aircraft is, where it was taken, and so on, but few people have that good a memory.

If you intend to sell your pictures, labelling is even more important. Magazine editors like to see at a glance what a picture is about, without having to ring you. No picture library will accept a photograph unless it is properly captioned. And relevant, useful information supplied with a picture can help to sell it.

The amount of information you can cram on depends on the type of photograph. With a print, a sheet of paper can be taped to the back. This is better than writing directly on the print for several reasons. Writing can show through when the picture is screened for reproduction. You might want to change the caption details at a later date. And some types of paper, particularly the now-common resin coated varieties, are difficult to write on anyway. If you are not likely to want to change the details, using self-adhesive labels is fine.

Things are a little more difficult when it comes to transparencies. You can write directly on to card mounts, although things get rather messy if you make mistakes. Alternatively, you can use small self-adhesive labels. You will have to use labels if the mounts are plastic.

There can be such a thing as too much information. It's a mistake to try to predict the requirements of everybody who is likely to look at the picture. The essential information boils down to this:

■ Your name (an absolute must) and, if possible, a means of contact, such as a telephone number.

■ The aircraft manufacturer, type and model number.

■ The aircraft owner.

■ Where the picture was taken.

■ When it was taken.

■ Any notable feature of the picture that might be overlooked (never assume the person looking at the picture is an aviation expert).

An example of this type of caption might be:

Chance Vought F4U-4 Corsair (Old Flying Machine Company). 'Wings of Victory' air show, Coventry Airport, Baginton, August 1988. © Steve Mansfield (Tel: 01-234 5678).

Note the use of the copyright symbol. Copyright is automatically yours (unless you were commissioned to take the pictures, where it can get a little hazy), but it's worth putting the symbol in, just to let people know. The caption might have to be abbreviated somewhat to fit it on the edge of a transparency mount. Normally, you can fit two lines of text quite comfortably on each of the two wider edges, which would boil down to something like:

Chance Vought F4U-4, Corsair (OFMC), 'Wings of Victory', Baginton, © Steve Mansfield 1988.

PROFILE:
CHARLES BROWN

Leafing through the photographs of Charles E. Brown is a sobering and humbling experience. Whatever new idea you think you may have, whatever new angle you think you've invented when it comes to photographing aircraft, Charles Brown has already been there and done it — decades ago.

Working from the early 1920s until retirement in the 1960s, Brown covered aircraft from just about every angle, civil and military, in the air and on the ground. It was a period which many consider to be a golden age of aviation, and Brown was its leading historian, his pictures capturing a vast variety of types, both famous and obscure.

HISTORY

For his fourteenth birthday, in 1910, he received his first camera, a small folding model. With it he took the picture that launched his career: the picture of a balloon was sold to the *Daily Mirror* where, two years later, the young Brown was hired for work in the darkrooms where he learned and perfected the technicalities of film processing and printing. He eventually graduated to assignments as a photographer. Although turned down by the photographic section of the Royal Naval Air Service, Brown was eventually drafted into the Royal Engineers, and in 1918–19 was also doing work for the Royal Air Force.

After the war, Brown continued as a press photographer, going freelance in 1921. Travel and steam locomotives were early specializations, but he quickly gravitated towards aircraft, which were continually grabbing the headlines. He photographed air shows and RAF air stations, quickly building a solid reputation.

It wasn't long before his talents were in great demand. He was invited to photograph prototypes and new aircraft. Brown assiduously built up contacts, both in the squadrons and in the relevant government departments. He developed strong relationships with the pilots; after all, he was forever putting his life in their hands. He trusted and relied on their skills and they responded by giving him all the help they could — flying when and where he wanted, throttling back at the right moment to reduce vibration, and so on. People enjoyed working with Brown and he made sure that everyone involved received prints from the session. This wasn't simply a matter of good manners, although that was certainly a strong element in Brown's character; he knew that getting his type of photographs depended on the whole-hearted co-operation of the flyers, ground crews and pencil pushers. And his thoughtfulness paid dividends: Brown was given access to machines, personnel and flying time that other photographers could only view with envy. This continued during his time, later in the war, as an official war correspondent assigned to the 2nd Tactical Air Force, and afterwards when he returned to civilian life as a freelance photographer.

The only hiccup in his career came when his office in the City was bombed. Precious photographs were destroyed, as many of them were glass plate negatives.

Charles Brown waits to take off in an Auster 6. Hanging out of the side of an aircraft with a bulky plate camera was a familiar situation for him

EQUIPMENT

Why Brown took photographs is not hard to divine. But how he took the pictures is a subject which may be greeted with some incredulity by subsequent generations of photographers raised on modern, sophisticated hardware.

His first professional camera, and one that remained a favourite throughout his career, was the Zeiss Palmos, a large, ugly brute by modern standards, taking large format plate film, one shot at a time in a film holder. It was equipped with a six-inch Taylor Hobson lens using helical focusing. The camera's cloth bellows was eventually replaced with wood; Brown noted, somewhat dryly, that the increased slipstream of faster, post-war aircraft had a tendency to 'blow in' the bellows. Towards the end of World War Two, while on assignment with the 2nd Tactical Air Force, he moved to a more compact 35 mm Zeiss Contax.

As far as film was concerned, Brown preferred to work with the fastest stock he could get hold of, and also liked to use glass plates rather than film-based stock.

The vast number of his black and white images tends to obscure the fact that Brown was also taking a lot of colour photographs. During World War Two colour film was hard to come by. Most of it was in the hands of the Americans and Brown made sure of his supply of Kodachrome and Ektachrome by accepting assignments for the US magazine, *Flying*. All the same, he would rarely take more than two or three shots of a subject.

Two Supermarine Southampton IIs over the Isle of Wight, sometime in the late 1920s. Charles Brown's career spans one of the finest agest of aviation, from lumbering biplanes to fast jets

TECHNIQUE

Whenever possible he avoided having glass or Perspex in the way. Often shots were taken from the rear turret of multi-engine aircraft such as the Lancaster. A couple of 1953 pictures show Brown and others in the rear of a USAF Fairchild C-119 Flying Boxcar, the rear doors removed, cameras mounted on tripods in the cavernous opening, and everyone wrapped warmly in flying jackets! Another has him hanging out the side of an Auster 6 facing backwards. It was techniques like this that allowed him to capture breathtaking head-on, air-to-air views.

Before take-off, Brown always had a good idea of where he wanted his target aircraft in relation to the camera ship, in order to get the best light. Once in the air, manoeuvring was co-ordinated with the aid of pre-arranged hand signals.

Brown's ground shots include mechanics working on aircraft, Lindbergh's aircraft after his famous Atlantic crossing, and so on, but his most spectacular photographs show aircraft in their natural element — airborne. Brown was not above the occasional touch of wit: a group shot of five Central Flying School Tiger Moths shows them inverted (they had recently been specially adapted for inverted flight). Others are simply stunning: his head-on shot of a Lightning is enough to make anyone draw breath. And many provoke nostalgia, sometimes fond, sometimes sad: a lone Lancaster above the clouds, its wings glinting from a low sun, can't help but evoke emotions, not least for those who were there at the time.

The prototype Hawker Hurricane, K5083, photographed in 1935. Charles Brown was there to record the early test flight of this famous fighter

For the aviation enthusiast, Brown's collection of pictures is a treasure trove, covering everything from the Fairey Flycatcher I to jet fighters like the Hawker Siddeley P.1127 Kestrel, the forerunner of the Harrier. Many of the types shown are no longer with us, and those that still exist are now often permanently grounded in museums, the aircraft unable to fly or their owners unwilling to risk them. Brown's pictures are our only reminder of how majestic, exciting and occasionally comical these aircraft could be in flight.

His standards were exacting. He knew what he wanted from each flight and would spend hours, if necessary, getting it. This set him apart from less demanding photographers and helped build his reputation for quality. And perhaps part of this reputation stems from Brown's insistence on authenticity. Like any other photographer, he would occasionally burn in skies when printing, or do a little artful dodging. But wholesale fabrication or modification of the image was out of the question. In one of his rare articles Brown says: 'Subsequent faking is but a disguise for a job improperly done.'

A lone Lancaster BII navigates the cloud tops. Probably the most famous bomber of World War Two, the Lanc was a frequent subject for Charles Brown, and he recorded most of the various models

Opposite: The need for careful co-ordination in the air is dramatically demonstrated by this shot of a Fairey Firefly F1. There is little room for mistakes with this kind of manoeuvre

Brown also developed something of a style. He liked to have cloud in the shot — if possible to be above it — as a way of introducing an interesting backdrop in place of what otherwise could be a drab sky (especially in black and white where you don't even have colour to help out). 'There is no more beautiful background,' he wrote. But going above the clouds had a practical benefit, too; in cloud-cloaked Britain it was way of getting into the sunshine.

Brown's main concern, however, was always for the aircraft itself — to get pictures so sharp and detailed that they could be used by technical departments and engineers for diagnosing faults.

In 1978, Brown's vast stock of photographs was taken under the wing of the Royal Air Force Museum in Hendon, London, where it is being catalogued and maintained as a valuable national resource. Charles Brown died in 1982, leaving behind a unique record of aviation history.

Shooting straight out of the back of the camera-ship allowed Charles Brown to get this spectacular view of a BAC Lightning T4

APPENDIX A

MAJOR UK & US AIR SHOWS

An air show is undoubtedly the easiest way of getting close to interesting aircraft. It would be impossible to list all shows — some are one-offs and most change their dates from time to time, in an attempt to accommodate popular holiday dates and perhaps have a stab at getting better weather. The following, brief, list indicates the major annual events, with a rough indication of the time of year in which they take place. For definite dates, keep an eye on aviation magazines, which often carry listings and give contact names and numbers.

Don't be fooled into thinking that only the large shows are worth attending. Local displays and fly-ins can be just as interesting, and you might stand a better chance of getting close to the aircraft. Also, many military bases hold open days, which are definitely worth attending. Finally, it should be noted that nothing in this world is permanent, and it is possible that some of these events may die a natural death, unlikely as it sounds.

UK

FIGHTER MEET
Mid-May, North Weald Airfield, Epping, Essex. One of the best gatherings of classic warbirds you will see in the UK.

BIGGIN HILL INTERNATIONAL AIR FAIR
Mid-June, Biggin Hill Airfield, Westerham, Kent. One of the biggest and best of the air shows — always has an entertaining mix of classic and modern aircraft.

SBAC FARNBOROUGH
Early September, Farnborough Airfield, Hampshire. As it is mainly a trade show, Farnborough is one of the best places to see the latest in hardware, often being put through its paces in thrilling displays. Try to get there on the press day, if you can, as the crowds are marginally lighter.

DUXFORD
Mid-September, Imperial War Museum, Duxford Airfield, Cambridge. An excellent blend of aerobatics, classic aircraft displays and military flypasts.

USA

VALIANT AIR COMMAND, TICO
Mid-March, Titusville, Florida. An off-shoot of the Confederate Air Force shows, the Tico meet is usually the first major event in the US air show season. It features mainly warbirds, from World War Two onwards.

EAA FLY-IN, OSHKOSH
Late July/early August (eight days), Wittman Field, Oshkosh, Wisconsin. The biggest airshow in the world in sheer number of aircraft, Oshkosh offers everything from vintage light aircraft through classic warbirds to the latest high-tech hardware. As it is officially the annual fly-in and convention of the Experimental Aircraft Association, the emphasis is on home-built and developmental types.

RENO AIR RACES
Mid-September, Stead Airfield, Reno, Nevada. Probably the most thrilling air show, the four days of the National Championship Air Races offer four classes of closed-circuit racing. The main attraction is the Unlimited class which features mainly modified warbirds — P-51s, Bearcats, Sea Furies et al. Plus aerobatic and military displays.

CONFEDERATE AIR FORCE AIRSHOW
Mid-October, Harlingen, Texas. An outing for one of the most unusual (and biggest!) air forces in the world. Classic warbirds being flown to their limits.

APPENDIX B
AIR MUSEUMS AND COLLECTIONS
UK

AEROSPACE MUSEUM
RAF Cosford, Wolverhampton, West Midlands WV7 3EX. Tel: (090722) 4872

Part of the Royal Air Force Museum Collection. In addition to military types, with some interesting prototypes and experimental aircraft, this is the home of the British Airways Collection.

BATTLE OF BRITAIN MEMORIAL FLIGHT
RAF Coningsby, Lincolnshire LN4 4SY. Tel: (0526) 42581

Viewing by special permission only. This is the RAF Museum Collection's flying display, including airworthy Spitfires, Hurricanes and a Lancaster.

FLEET AIR ARM MUSEUM
Royal Naval Air Station, Yeovilton, Ilchester, Somerset BA22 8HT. Tel: (0935) 840551

The Fleet Air Arm Museum has become one of the most important collections in the country. Opening times vary depending on the time of year, so it's wise to ring before you visit.

IMPERIAL WAR MUSEUM, DUXFORD
Duxford Airfield, Duxford, Cambridgeshire CB2 4QR. Tel: (0223) 833963

On the site of one of the key World War Two aerodromes, the Imperial War Museum's Duxford museum is one of the most important collections in the country. Permanent exhibits are nicely complemented by a continually changing variety of privately-owned types.

MOSQUITO AIRCRAFT MUSEUM
Salisbury Hall, London Colney, St Albans, Hertfordshire AL2 1BU. Tel: (0727) 22051

This is where the Mosquito was born, with many early flights taking off from adjacent fields. The original prototype is accompanied by other Mosquitos and an elegant collection of (mainly) de Havilland aircraft. Not open all year, so check before going.

MUSEUM OF ARMY FLYING
Army Air Corps Centre, Middle Wallop, Stockbridge, Hampshire SO20 8DY.
Tel: (0264) 62121

An unusual collection covering the spectrum of army flying, from Horsa gliders to Argentinean Pucaras captured in the Falklands, plus what is possibly the oldest surviving helicopter — Raoul Hafner's R.II.

ROYAL AIR FORCE MUSEUM
BATTLE OF BRITAIN MUSEUM
BOMBER COMMAND MUSEUM
Hendon, London NW9 5LL. Tel: 01-205 2266

Housed in one complex within easy striking distance of Central London, these three important collections are imaginatively and strikingly displayed.

SCIENCE MUSEUM
Exhibition Road, South Kensington, London SW7 2DD. Tel: 01-589 3456

With the emphasis on technical development, the collection displays a broad range of aircraft, from the earliest to the latest. Also has an excellent collection of engines.

SHUTTLEWORTH COLLECTION
Old Warden Aerodrome, Biggleswade, Bedfordshire SG18 9ER. Tel: (0767) 27288

The main strength of this collection is in World War One and inter-war types. Most of the exhibits are in flying condition and are regularly displayed, both at Old Warden and other shows around the country.

ST ATHAN HISTORIC AIRCRAFT COLLECTION
RAF St Athan, Barry, South Glamorgan CF6 9WA. Tel: (04465) 3131

The highlights of the collection are rare Axis aircraft, including unique examples of the Mitsubishi Ki 46 and the Kawasaki Ki 100.

USA

UNITED STATES ARMY AVIATION MUSEUM
Fort Rucker, Alabama 36360. Tel: 205-255 4507

A vast collection with a particularly wide (and occasionally weird) selection of helicopters. Claimed to be the largest collection of choppers in the world.

CHAMPLIN FIGHTER MUSEUM
4636 Figher Aces Drive, Mesa, Arizona 85205. Tel: 602-830 4540

A fascinating collection of World War One aircraft (including many flying replicas), plus an interesting selection of World War Two German types, including a Focke-Wulf FW 190D.

PIMA AIR MUSEUM
6400 South Wilmot Road, Tucson, Arizona 85706. Tel: 602-574 0462

An off-shoot of the USAF's storage facility at Davis-Monthan Air Force Base, this huge collection spans all types, from fighters to bombers and transports.

PLANES OF FAME
7000 Merrill Avenue, Chino Airport, California 91710. Tel: 714-597 3722

An excellent collection, with the emphasis on fighters, and most in flying condition. Worth turning up at any time — almost obligatory on display days.

CASTLE AIR MUSEUM
Castle Air Force Base, Atwater, California 95342. Tel: 209-726 2011

The accent here is on American bombers. The museum has an impressive array of World War Two types.

MARCH FIELD MUSEUM
March Air Force Base, California 92518. Tel: 714-655 3725

A fast-expanding collection which includes training and liaison types alongside World War Two bombers and early jets.

SAN DIEGO AEROSPACE MUSEUM
2001 Pan American Plaza, Balboa Park, San Diego, California 92101. Tel: 619-234 8291

A large collection of early types, including many rarities, plus a smattering of World War Two and more recent aircraft.

NEW ENGLAND AIR MUSEUM
Bradley International Airport, Windsor Locks, Connecticut 06096. Tel: 203-623 3305

A vast collection covering all eras of aviation and all types, from warbirds to ultralites.

NATIONAL AIR & SPACE MUSEUM
Smithsonian Institution, Washington, District of Columbia 20560.
Tel: 202-357 3133

Undoubtedly one of the best, and biggest, collections in the world. The museum displays a huge variety of types, including many historic and famous aircraft, although this is only a fraction of the total collection, as many of the exhibits are in storage or on loan to other museums.

NAVAL AVIATION MUSEUM
Pensacola Naval Air Station, Florida 32508. Tel: 904-452 3543

The collection covers the development of US Navy aviation, including fighters, flying boats, bombers and helicopters.

WEEKS AIR MUSEUM
14710 SW 128th Street, Miami, Florida 33186.

The private collection of top aerobatic pilot Kermit Weeks. The acquisitive Mr Weeks has put together a fascinating assortment of warbirds, including fighters and bombers.

ROBINS AFB MUSEUM OF AVIATION
Warner Robins, Georgia 31099. Tel: 912-926 6870

Another fast-growing museum, which prides itself on its restoration record. Exhibits are mainly military types, including early jet fighters.

AIRPOWER MUSEUM
Antique Airfield, Ottumwa, Iowa 52501. Tel: 515-938 2773

Run in conjunction with the Antique Airplane Association, the museum has an unusual collection of mostly inter-war types, with many in flying condition.

COMBAT AIR MUSEUM
Forbes Field, Topeka, Kansas 66619. Tel: 913-862 9649

Concerned mainly with restoring and displaying aircraft representing the US at war, the museum maintains a collection of flyable machines, in addition to the static exhibits.

HENRY FORD MUSEUM
The Edison Institute, 20900 Oakwood Boulevard, Dearborn, Michigan 48121. Tel: 313-271 1620

The museum complex includes the Greenfield Village, replicating life at the turn of the century, including a replica of the Wright brothers' bicycle shop. Aircraft exhibits, which concentrate on early types, naturally include the Ford Flivver and Tri-Motor.

PLANES OF FAME EAST
14771 Pioneer Trail, Eden Prairie, Minnesota 55344. Tel: 612-941 2633

The small but perfectly formed private collection of Bob Pond, mostly comprising World War Two fighters and with an emphasis on Navy types. All the aircraft are flyable and displayed regularly.

STRATEGIC AIR COMMAND MUSEUM
2510 Clay Street, Belleville, Nebraska 68005. Tel: 402-292 2001

As you might expect, bombers feature heavily here, although there are interesting fighter and transport aircraft.

CRADLE OF AVIATION MUSEUM
Mitchel Field, Garden City, New York 11530. Tel: 516-222 1191

Alongside the more familiar fighter types, housed in this Long Island museum, are many unusual and rare aircraft, including Lindbergh's first aircraft — a Curtiss Jenny. May be closed during winter months.

INTREPID SEA-AIR-SPACE MUSEUM
Intrepid Square, W 46th Street and 12th Avenue, New York City, New York 10036. Tel: 212-245 2533

Manhatten isn't an obvious place for an aircraft museum. What's even more surprising is that it's housed on an aircraft carrier. The collection includes a good selection of Navy jets.

OLD RHINEBECK AERODROME
Rhinebeck, New York 12572. Tel: 914-758 8610

One of the most popular museums, not least for its regular air shows. The collection includes a large selection of pre-1930 types.

WRIGHT BROTHERS MUSEUM/FIRST FLIGHT
4-7 Kill Devil Hill, North Carolina 27948. Tel: (919) 441-7430

Not much in the way of aircraft to photograph, but the importance of the location warrants its inclusion here. The best way to see it is to fly in. There is a small charge for parking your aircraft which includes access to the monument, perched atop the overgrown sand dune from which the Wright brothers made their first experimental glides, and the museum. This contains replicas of the earliest craft, while outside are markers showing the ground covered by the first four flights, and replicas of the huts in which the Wrights lived and worked.

UNITED STATES AIR FORCE MUSEUM
Wright Patterson Air Force Base, Ohio 45433. Tel: 513-255 3284

A huge and immensely popular museum which seems to include one of everything that the USAF ever flew, plus a lot besides. One of the top collections in the world — an absolute must.

CONFEDERATE AIR FORCE FLYING MUSEUM
Harlingen International Airport, Texas 78551. Tel: 512-425 1057

One of the most famous outfits in the world, the CAF attempts to maintain a flyable collection of all US combat aircraft — at least of World War Two vintage — as well as the more famous foreign types. Justly renowned for their lively air shows, the CAF is an act not to be missed.

TEXAS MUSEUM OF MILITARY HISTORY
Dyess Air Force Base, Texas 79607. Tel: 915-696 2121

The aircraft are part of a museum which includes military vehicles, weapons and ships. The collection includes a good selection of US bombers and jet fighters.

USAF HISTORY AND TRADITIONS MUSEUM
Lackland Air Force Base, Texas 78236. Tel: 512-671 3444

A large collection which includes a wide variety of jet fighters, plus bombers, transports and trainers.

MARINE CORPS AIR-GROUND MUSEUM
Quantico, Virginia 22134. Tel: 703-640 2606

A large collection of aircraft, dating mainly from World War Two onwards, with an impressive array of fighters.

MUSEUM OF FLIGHT
9404 East Marginal Way South, Seattle, Washington 98108. Tel: 206-767 7373

Located at the edge of Boeing Field, one might expect the museum to be dominated by the company. However, although Boeing is well represented — from replicas of its early output to the Flying Fortress and Stratojet — the collection is varied and surprising, ranging from the Curtiss Jenny to the Rutan Vari-Eze.

EXPERIMENTAL AIRCRAFT ASSOCIATION MUSEUM
3000 Poberezny Road, Wittman Field, Oshkosh, Wisconsin 54903. Tel: 414-426 4818

As home of the Experimental Aircraft Association and its annual fly-in, you would expect this vast and beautiful collection to have more than its fair share of weird and wonderful types — and you wouldn't be disappointed. But it also has many classics, including military aircraft.

APPENDIX C
THE LAWS OF AVIATION PHOTOGRAPHY

With any luck, the advice in this book will help you overcome the biggest problems involved in photographing aircraft. However, life is less than perfect, and there are certain laws to which even the most experienced and talented professional is subject:

- The lens you need is always the one in the bag.
- The filter you need is always on another lens.
- You always have the wrong film in the camera.
- In a motordrive sequence, the best picture is always between two frames.
- Exciting events always take place while you are changing film.
- The *most* exciting events take place after you have run out of film.
- You are always closer to the end of the film than you thought.
- You always have one roll of film less than you thought.
- On a tripod, there is always one leg extension you forgot to tighten.
- Lost or damaged films always have the best shots on them.

And with apologies to Sir Isaac Newton:

- An aeroplane will continue in a straight line until a split second before you hit the shutter release.
- The rate at which an aeroplane continually moves out of the frame is proportional to how much you want to photograph it, and its direction is entirely unpredictable.
- For every action there is someone's head in the way.

APPENDIX D
FURTHER READING

In any field of photography, it's a good idea to know your subject. Some kind of spotter's book should help you to identify the more common aircraft types.

Even if you are not a pilot and have no intention of becoming one, a flying primer — the sort of thing read by people embarking on a private pilot's licence course — will help you understand what's going on, and will help you to communicate more effectively with pilots. This can be essential if you are trying to set up some kind of air-to-air shoot. And if you intend to use an airband scanner or transceiver, a manual on radiotelephony procedures should help you to translate the jargon.

A simple volume on meteorology can prove to be worth its weight in gold. The aviation photographer is a victim of the weather, and by getting to know the various kinds of weather systems — what a warm front or cold front implies and how to interpret weather maps and forecasts — you can avoid wasting time and money setting up sorties or trips to airfields on days that are likely to be socked-in.

Even pictures books and magazines are useful. Look at the photographs and try to work out what the photographers did. Look closely at the lighting angle, and try to judge the length of the lens (it's usually possible to get a rough idea).

Getting hold of a 'quarter mill' (1:250,000 scale) aviation chart of your local area will help you find your local airfields, and it will look highly impressive on your study wall. Other goodies to pick up from the shop at the airfield include a list of communication frequencies used in your country and guides to airfields (which usually include telephone numbers).

APPENDIX E
GLOSSARY

Aperture
This is literally a hole in the lens. A variable aperture, or iris, like the pupils in your eyes, controls the amount of light coming through the lens. Making the hole smaller cuts down the amount of light, while opening it up increases the level of the light transmitted. In theory, the number you set on the ring — $f2.8$, $f8$ or whatever — indicates how many times the actual aperture, the hole, fits into the focal length of the lens. So the smaller the number, the larger the hole and the more the amount of light. A physical limit is imposed by the size of the lens barrel, which is why fast versions of lenses have large diameter front elements.

Depth of field
This is the area extending either side of the main point of focus (both towards and away from the camera) in which objects are also sharp. It varies according to several parameters, increasing with shorter focal length lenses, smaller apertures and more distant focus points.

Depth of focus
This is the area either side of the image plane (where the film sits) in which the image still appears sharp. A large depth of focus is useful for avoiding problems with film flatness or positioning.

DX coding
A system by which the camera can automatically set the film speed. DX-coded films have a rectangular pattern of black and silver squares painted on the cassette. Prongs inside the camera contact with the squares and can read the pattern electrically (only the silver squares conduct electricity).

Exposure Metering
Average: This system reads all parts of the subject equally and gives an overall exposure. It assumes that there is an even distribution of tones.

Spot: This system reads just a small part of the subject. It is best used when the tonal distribution is uneven. The most important tones can be metered in isolation.

Multi-pattern: An increasingly popular feature of modern SLR cameras, multi-pattern metering measures several parts of the scene and compares the distribution of tones with an internal database. It can recognise uneven tone patterns and expose accordingly. Although not foolproof, it is more accurate than other methods and so is normally used in conjunction with automatic exposure systems.

Incident: This is where the light falling onto the subject, rather than the light reflected from it, is measured. Usually carried out using a hand-held meter placed near the subject, it is accurate because it is not affected by the colour or tone of the subject.

Film speed: *see* **Speed.**

Flash synchronization

This is most critical with focal plane shutters. The duration of the flash light is so short that it must be timed to occur when the shutter is fully open, if the whole frame is to be exposed. When the shutter speed becomes so fast that the shutter is like a slit moving across the image, flash photography becomes impossible, as there is no time when the shutter is fully open. The flash sync speed is the fastest speed which can be used with flash, and is typically in the region of 1/60th–1/125th.

Focal plane shutter

Various types of shutter are used in cameras. By far the most common type in 35 mm SLRs is the focal plane variety. It gets its name from the fact that it sits close to where the image is focused — that is, on the film. It works by using two blinds, with the first normally closed. When you trip the shutter release, the first blind opens, allowing light to fall on the film. After the allotted time (the shutter speed or exposure time) the second blind closes, shutting out the light. With short exposures — around 1/125th and faster — the second blind starts to close before the first is fully open, so the two blinds effectively form a slit moving across the frame.

Lenses

Fast: A fast lens is one which has an unusually large maximum aperture. For example, a normal maximum aperture for a 300 mm lens is $f4.5$, but versions are available which have apertures of $f2.8$. The advantages of fast lenses are: snappier and easier focusing; ability to get pictures in lower light; and the ability to use faster shutter speeds for less camera shake. The disadvantages are size, weight and cost.

Telephoto: A longer than normal lens with a narrow angle of view. It magnifies the scene to allow the photographer to select just a small part of it. True telephoto designs use special optical techniques to make the lens itself shorter than its focal length, to make it more practical. This distinguishes telephotos from 'long focus' lenses.

Varifocal: A simple kind of zoom lens (see below), but one where accurate focus is not maintained as the focal length is changed.

Wide angle: Lenses with a wide angle of view, often used to get a whole subject in the frame when it isn't possible to get back far enough to use longer lenses. The perspective effects created by this close-up viewpoint can be very dramatic.

Zooms: These lenses allow the focal length to be continuously varied over a given range, e.g. 35–70 mm. The advantage is that one lens can replace several fixed focal length lenses. Disadvantages usually include weight, speed and cost. True zooms maintain focus when the focal length is altered.

Speed

Of film: This is a measure of how sensitive the film is to light. 'Faster' films, which have higher ISO or DIN numbers, require less exposure, and so allow faster shutter speeds and/or smaller apertures. The trade-off is that they are usually less sharp and not so capable of resolving fine detail.

Of lens: The speed of a lens refers to its maximum aperture. A typical standard (50 mm) lens for a 35 mm SLR has a speed of $f1.8$. Lenses with large maximum apertures are said to be 'fast' while others are 'slow'. As the aperture number is worked out by dividing the size of the hole into the length of the lens, long lenses tend to be slower. Lenses which need to cover a larger area of film also tend to be slower. *See also*: **Lenses, Fast.**

Of shutter: The shutter speed refers to the amount of time for which light is allowed to fall on the film. It is worth noting that in the type of shutter found in 35 mm SLRs, the focal plane shutter, not all of the film is exposed at once (see **Focal Plane Shutter**).

Single Lens Reflex: A type of camera in which viewing is done through the same lens which is used to take the picture. This is normally achieved by having a mirror just behind the lens, reflecting the image on to a screen. This image is reversed laterally, but most 35 mm SLRs have a prism viewfinder which corrects this, and gives a line-of-sight viewing angle. Medium format SLRs usually have prism viewfinders available as an option. When the shutter release is pressed, the mirror swings out of the way just prior to the shutter opening. In modern cameras, the mirror returns immediately after the shutter closes, although some older types and medium format SLRs have 'non-return' mirrors which are cranked back into place when the film is advanced.

SLR: *see* **Single Lens Reflex.**

Stop

In a sense, this is the standard unit of photographic exposure. The term is largely interchangeable with 'aperture', although it has a slightly larger meaning. Whereas aperture refers directly to the size of the hole, stop refers to the setting. You can talk about 'opening up a stop', when you move to the next largest aperture setting, e.g. $f8$ to $f5.6$. The term is also used to denote general exposure settings. To say a picture has been 'over-exposed by one stop' could mean that it was shot at, say, $f4$ instead of the correct $f5.6$, but it could equally mean it was shot at 1/60th instead of 1/125th, with the aperture remaining the same. In this respect its meaning is very similar to exposure values (EVs). The EV scale is a general way of describing exposure level, and some light meters use it. The meter gives a reading of, say, EV10, and it's then up to you to decide how you want to achieve this value in the camera — which combination of shutter speed and aperture you wish to use.

Telephoto: *See* **Lenses.**

Through-the-Lens

This term applies to light metering and viewing. A camera which uses TTL viewing is, in other words, a single lens reflex. TTL metering, where electronic light cells measure the light reaching the focusing screen, reflected from the film or travelling through a semi-silvered section of the mirror, is now a common way for SLR camera systems to determine correct exposure. It is generally accurate because it measures only the light forming the final image. TTL flash metering is also common now: this is where the duration of the light from the flashgun is controlled by the camera, which measures it during the exposure. Special 'dedicated' flash units are required.

TTL: *See* **Through-the-Lens.**

Wide Angle: *See* **Lenses.**

Zoom: *See* **Lenses.**